MORE CIRCULAR DORSET WALKS

BY

EDWARD GRIFFITHS

ANOTHER SET OF GUIDED WALKS
FOR AN INTIMATE EXPLORATION OF
THE BEST OF DORSET

INCLUDES HISTORICAL DETAILS OF PLACES VISITED

Jog on, jog on, the footpath way,
And merrily hent the stile-a:
A merry heart goes all the day,
Your sad tires in a mile-a.

Autolycus, The Winter's Tale
William Shakespeare

BY THE SAME AUTHOR

THE STOUR VALLEY WAY   ISBN 0 9530338 2 1

The Official Guide to the National Long-Distance Trail - in association with Dorset County Council, North Dorset District Council, The Stour Valley Project, The Countryside Agency and Greenlink

THE CRANBORNE CHASE PATH   ISBN 0 9519376 2 6

"....the anecdotes and passionate descriptions will delight even those familiar with the Chase".....Western Gazette

THE BLACKMORE VALE PATH   ISBN 0 9519376 3 4

"....a walk to be savoured.   Happy rambling and enjoy Dorset".....Blackmore Vale Magazine

CIRCULAR DORSET RAMBLES   ISBN 0 9530338 4 8

"...reflects the diversity of landscape and beauty of the county....you won't be disappointed".....Country Walking

HILL WALKING IN DORSET   ISBN O 9530338 0 5

Circular walks to 20 Dorset peaks.   "Climb the equivalent of three Scafell Pikes without leaving Dorset".

ALL RIGHTS RESERVED   FIRST PUBLISHED - 2000

C EDWARD R GRIFFITHS

ISBN 0 9530338 3 X

Published by Green Fields Books
13 Dalewood Avenue, Bear Cross
Bournemouth, BH11 9NR

CONTENTS

Front cover photograph - Spetisbury and the River Stour from Crawford Bridge

Title Reverse picture - Stag Gate, Charborough Park.   Page 52

WALKS IN THIS BOOK

1 LANGTON MATRAVERS

ROUTE 1 -   5 MILES - Field and cliff paths and some undulating stony tracks through quarries.

ROUTE 2 -   5 MILES - Field paths and farm tracks, hills and dales.

2 STURMINSTER NEWTON

ROUTE 1 -   6.3/4 MILES - Field paths, tracks and country lanes through villages and past mills.

ROUTE 2 -   4 MILES - As Route 1 but shorter.

3 STURMINSTER MARSHALL

8.1/4 MILES - Undulating field paths and tracks to hill fort, woods and mills.

4 THROOP AND PARLEY

5.3/4 MILES - Field paths and tracks along River Stour.   Can be muddy after rain.

5 PIDDLETRENTHIDE AND PLUSH

5.1/4 MILES - Hills and valleys (some steep) on field paths and tracks

6 SPETISBURY

3.1/2 MILES - Hill fort, meadows, River Stour flood plain and Abbey tracks.   Can be muddy after rain.

7. WIMBORNE STOUR

ROUTE 1 -   7.1/2 MILES - Some easy walking on tarmac and level field paths.   Two small elevations from Stour to Pamphill.   Stour path muddy after rain.

ROUTE 2 -   4.3/4 MILES - Direct route into country.

8. BERE REGIS

ROUTE 1 -   3.1/4 MILES - Undulating field and heath walking on paths and tracks.   A little on country lanes.

ROUTE 2 -   6 MILES - As Route 1 but longer.

ROUTE 3 -   9.3/4 MILES - Even longer but the best.

9. SUTTON POYNTZ

5 MILES - Dry chalk hill walking but track down into Osmington can be muddy.

WALKS LOCATION MAP

1. LANGTON MATRAVERS AND ACTON
2. STURMINSTER NEWTON
3. STURMINSTER MARSHALL
4. THROOP AND PARLEY
5. PIDDLETRENTHIDE AND PLUSH
6. SPETISBURY
7. WIMBORNE STOUR
8. BERE REGIS
9. SUTTON POYNTZ

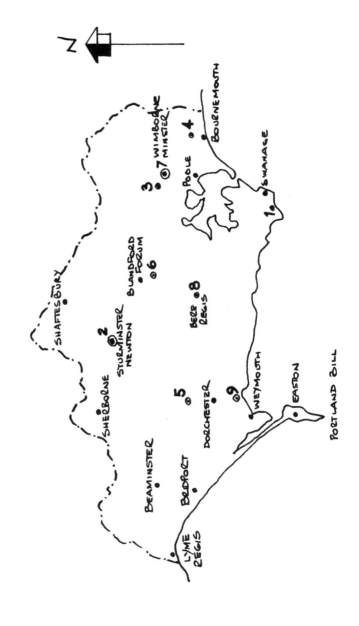

1

INTRODUCTION

"Another guided walks book?", I hear you say.   "We can walk wherever we like now, can't we?"   Well, maybe we can and maybe we can't (the finer details of the 'Right to Roam' legislation have still to be thrashed out) but where will you go to find the best walks and the most interesting days out.   Just ambling about willy-nilly won't be very satisfying.   That is exactly what the late, great explorer and curmudgeon, Alfred Wainwright referred to as 'aimless wandering'.

Anyway, the ancient paths and bridleways that we enjoy as Public Rights of Way didn't appear by accident.   They were established over generations as people went about their daily business, walking to work in the fields or great houses, working on church building or restoration, carrying goods of all kinds on pack horses or driving cattle and sheep to market, strolling in little family groups to church, hurrying daily from cottage to quarry and back and walking more carefully in their best finery to the annual fair on the village green or the harvest supper at the 'big house'.   Wouldn't it be a dreadful shame and a reflection on ourselves if these historic paths with so many memories stored under our feet were to disappear in the first years of the new millennium through our neglect and lack of use.   Future generations wouldn't thank us if the lovely system of paths and ancient tracks which we enjoy freely today could only be found then in some studiously researched 'Lost Paths of Dorset' book (or web site).

Another simple reason for using the old paths, especially when someone tells you in a book where they are, is that you can put your whole energy into enjoying where you are going and what you are seeing, rather then wasting time and effort wandering about huge fields trying to find not just any way out but the right way out so that you can continue the walk back to your starting point without a worry in the world.   Free time in the fresh air is precious enough without spoiling it with the stress of getting lost.

Finding a new walk is a rewarding experience but not everybody has the time to search out previously untried walks, in the hope that there will be good views and interesting things to see on the way.   A day out in the country is something to be savoured and, if the walk is a disappointment because the route is hard to find and the views are hidden because you find yourself in country lanes or sunken paths for a long way, it can spoil a whole weekend or put you off going out another time.

The walks in this book are some of the very best in Dorset with a good variety of beautiful landscapes and with interesting features to interest the whole family. Many more planned walks were tried but not included in this book for one reason or another.   For example, a route around Cranborne and Castle Hill was followed but much of it was on sunken tracks through ancient woodland.   Whilst the trees and birds are a source of much pleasure, most of the 5 miles had little in the way of views so, with the myriad of pleasures on the other walks pressing so hard for inclusion, Cranborne didn't quite make it.

All of the maps in this book are highly detailed so you shouldn't have any trouble finding your way but, if you do happen to wander off the route, maybe to see an exceptional view or to explore an adjacent path, the relevant Ordnance Survey maps which I recommend for each walk will soon bring you back.

The walks are all circular and all begin at a suitable spot where you can leave a car. However, if you would like to use public transport, various bus companies serve the areas in which you will be walking and the relevant bus nos. are listed in the introduction to each walk. The most used will be Wilts and Dorset, First Southern National and the independent operators whose timetables are listed in the booklets of 'Public Transport in Rural Dorset' which are obtainable from Tourist Information Centres throughout Dorset. These timetables, which give full addresses and telephone numbers of the operators, are also available from Environmental Services Directorate, Dorset County Council, County Hall, Dorchester, DT1 1XJ.

CIRCULAR WALKS IN THIS BOOK

Each walk begins with a description of the main features which you will meet during the day, together with the Map Reference for the starting point, the Ordnance Survey map/s which you should carry, parking areas available and the buses which will take you there. There are Mileage Tables and highly detailed Stage Maps which show you how far you have come from the start. Follow the Maps but don't miss the adjacent text because that is where you'll find the extra details that will add to your enjoyment of the walk.

"REMEMBER THE COUNTRY CODE".

Now, what should or shouldn't you do when you venture out into the countryside? I know you don't need me to remind you that, if you find a gate open, leave it open but otherwise you should always close gates behind you. We are only visitors in the countryside, especially in arable and pasture land, so take care of it. *Don't* drop litter and *do* respect the privacy of those whose cottage doorways you pass. Admiration is one thing - intrusion is another.

One point that is raised sometimes is, 'What if the way is blocked but there is an arrow pointing in a different direction?'. Routes of Footpaths and Bridleways can be changed at the request of landowners, farmers or individuals for many different reasons. This is an ongoing state of affairs and changes can be made even as a new book is going into print. So, if you find a change which is accompanied by clear signs and/or waymarks, follow the changed route (usually only over a short distance) until it rejoins your route. Any unauthorised changes or problems should be reported to the Rights of Way Section at Dorset County Council, Dorchester - Telephone 01305-224463

When parking the car, make sure that you don't block any access or cause a hazard in a country lane and don't assume that pub car parks are for general use. They are for customers so, even if you intend to have an expensive meal when you return, ask for permission before you leave your car in the car park.

Now, wearing the recommended footwear (I *always* wear hiking boots for good grip and to protect the ankles on rutted tracks) and carrying enough waterproofs to be prepared for the caprices of the English weather, get ready to go out and thoroughly enjoy yourself on this fine selection of More Circular Dorset Walks.

KEY TO MAP SYMBOLS

ROUTE	
MILES FROM START	
ADJOINING MAP NUMBER	
FOOTPATH OR BRIDLEWAY ARROW	
SIGNPOST	
HEDGE	
WIRE FENCE	
WOOD/IRON FENCE	
STONE/BRICK WALL	
STILE	
GATE - LARGE / SMALL	
TREE - DECIDUOUS / PINE	
SPECIFIC BUILDING	
GROUP OF BUILDINGS (schematic)	
TUMULUS/BARROW	
STREAM/RIVER	
BRIDGE OVER STREAM	
CLIFF EDGE	
GRADIENT (arrows point down)	
OVERHEAD CABLES	

PART ONE - AROUND LANGTON MATRAVERS

INTRODUCTION

After years and years of visiting the Isle of Purbeck and walking its miles of Footpaths, no excuse to go there again can ever be allowed to pass by. Purbeck was designed by natural forces but changed forever by the labours of man.   The rolling ridges of chalk and limestone have been quarried since time immemorial and the highly polished fossiliferous limestone was much prized as the nearest thing to marble without having to go to Connemara or even Italy. Lustrous, dark grey columns of Purbeck marble grace innumerable churches throughout the land, none more elegantly than those in Salisbury Cathedral. Rather alarmingly, those which complement the huge Chilmark stone columns below the tower and spire have bowed and twisted under the massive 6400 tons of stone which they are jointly supporting.

Langton Matravers runs either side of the B3069.   It is on Wilts and Dorset's frequent bus routes 142, 143 and 144 from Swanage to Poole and Bournemouth via Kingston and Corfe Castle.   The start for Route 1 is only 1/4 mile from the bus stop at Durnford Drove in the village itself and the start for Route 2 is within 20 yards of the bus stop at the Acton turning, 1/2 mile out of the village.

THE ALTERNATIVES

ROUTE 1: Total distance 5.1/4 miles - The first walk takes you to the Coast Path to visit some of the old quarries and to enjoy the magnificent cliff scenery in between.   You can explore the abandoned workings and visit the old quarrying villages of Langton and Worth Matravers.   The walk starts and ends in the National Trust's 'Spyway Farm' parking area along Durnford Drove at Ref. SY997784 on O S Map No. 195. This delightful walk leads you through the farm and down to Dancing Ledge and a long-deserted cliff-edge quarry.   Two miles of wonderful clifftop walking bring you through or past Seacombe Quarry and Winspit Quarry, both of which clearly demonstrate to those with imaginations exactly how difficult it must have been to win the precious stone from such an exposed and dangerous environment.   Turning inland, a visit to Worth Matravers, its church and its tea room (or the Square and Compass) is followed by an easy stroll along the Priests' Way back to the start.

ROUTE 2: Total distance 5.1/4 miles - This Route starts from a little free car park a few yards South of the B3069 bus stop and telephone box, in the turning for 'Acton'.   O.S. Ref SY989776.   This lovely walk takes you away from the busier parts of Purbeck and leads you along some intriguing ancient paths and tracks through beautiful dairy farming land.   It leads past fine 17thC farmhouses and passes under and over the Swanage Railway with its good collection of rescued steam trains that run regular services.   It has no strenuous hills yet there seem to be very few level surfaces all the way round.   Along the way, there are superb views of Corfe Castle, the surrounding ridges and distant Swanage. After all of these attractions, the walk meanders through the National Trust's old Wilkswood coppice before ending back at the little car park.

STAGE	MILES	TOTAL MILES
ROUTE 1:		
1 Durnford Drove to Spyway Farm	.75	.75
2 Spyway Farm to Eastington	.75	1.5
3 Eastington to Seacombe	.75	2.25
4 Seacombe to Winspit	.5	2.75
5 Winspit to Worth Matravers	.5	3.25
6 Worth Matravers to Abbascombe Farm	.5	3.75
7 Abbascombe Farm to Durnford Drove	1.5	**5.25**
ROUTE 2:		
1 Acton Car park to Haycraft Lane	1	1
2 Haycraft Lane to Woodyhyde Farm	.75	1.75
3 Woodyhyde Farm to Little Woolgarston	1	2.75
4 Little Woolgarston to Westwood Farm	.75	3.50
5 Westwood Farm to Wilkswood	1	4.50
6 Wilkswood to Acton Car Park	.75	**5.25**

Duck pond at Worth Matravers - Page 18

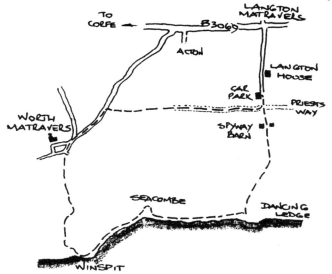

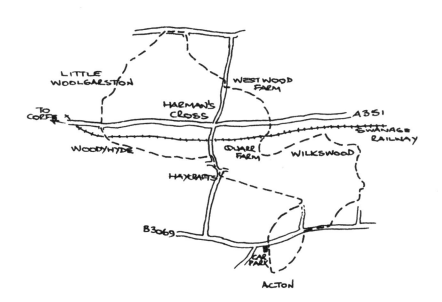

7

ROUTE 1 - STAGE 1

DURNFORD DROVE TO SPYWAY FARM

This walk starts in the National Trust's parking area on the 'Spyway Farm' estate but the first part of this map shows you how, when you get to the turning circle at the end of Durnford Drove, there is a gate onto the rough track that leads to the parking area.   To all intents and purposes, it looks as if the drive is private but it isn't.   Having said that, it may become a pay car park in the future if the National Trust find that it is getting too popular.   It is already much used by cliff climbers, walkers, bird watchers, geologists, young men who like jumping off cliffs into the sea (at Dancing Ledge) and others of a similar freedom-seeking persuasion.

Leave the parking area by going through the kissing gate in the stone wall and walking further up the track.   Immediately, there are fine views over the wall on your left to the Isle of Wight and Ballard Down.   The other high downland over your left shoulder is Nine Barrow Down and the gap between the two downs allows the road from Swanage to Studland and the Sandbanks Ferry to pass through. Take the grassy path to the right of the track as this is easier on the feet.

At the first junction of tracks, cross straight over the Priests' Way which runs from Worth Matravers to Swanage.   The first stone marker shows that it is 3/4 mile to Dancing Ledge.   The second shows that it is 1.1/2 miles to Worth and that particular section of the Priests' Way is your return route.   Turn off the track and cross the field diagonally towards the barns and cottage of Spyway Farm, almost parallel with the overhead electricity wires.

Go through the kissing gate into the farmyard and head for the low, corrugated iron-roofed barn where you will find a cluster of information boards extolling the natural and quarrying virtues of Dancing Ledge and the National Trust's surrounding lands.   Then, keep straight on through the next kissing gate into a high, level field with stone walls on either flank.

Cross the field on a grassy track to a field gate and pass into the next high field.

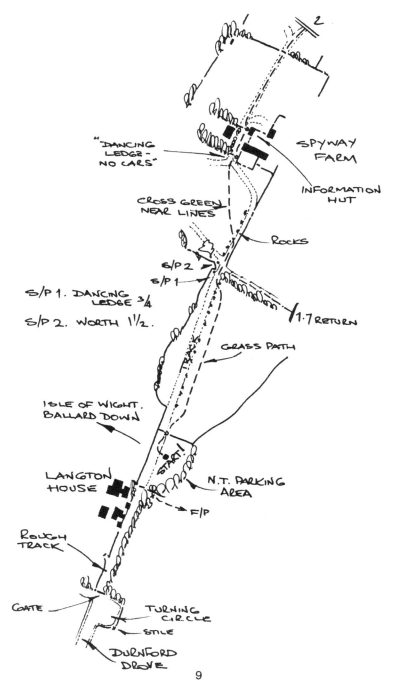

"DANCING
LEDGE -
NO CARS"

SPYWAY
FARM

INFORMATION
HUT

CROSS GREEN
NEAR LINES

ROCKS

S/P 2

S/P 1

S/P 1. DANCING
LEDGE 3/4

S/P 2. WORTH 1½.

1.7 RETURN

GRASS PATH

ISLE OF WIGHT.
BALLARD DOWN

LANGTON
HOUSE

START

N.T. PARKING
AREA

F/P

ROUGH
TRACK

GATE

TURNING
CIRCLE

STILE

DURNFORD
DROVE

9

ROUTE 1 - STAGE 2

SPYWAY FARM TO EASTINGTON

As you cross the field, the views begin to open out ahead and the sea which will be your companion for the next 2 miles stretches away to the wide, curved horizon. Go through the kissing gate and stay awhile on the top of the downs near the stone which points you down to 'Dancing Ledge'. Drink in the air and the view before beginning your descent on the stone steps which have been built into the hillside to resist the erosion caused by your - and thousands of other - feet.

As the gradient eases, the steps are no longer necessary and a smooth, grassy slope leads you down to a pair of stiles over to Dancing Ledge and a gap in the stone wall on your right. This is a walk of exploration so go over a stile and enjoy a few moments in the old quarry.

The quarry gets its name from the horizontal shelf of rock which is covered by the sea at high tide. In its more gentle mood, the retreating waves run over this shelf and the bumps and hollows in its surface cause the waves to foam and 'dance'. The rectangular pool is said to have been blasted out to allow local school-children to have somewhere safe to swim. Similarly, it is also said that it was a place to load stone onto a small boat when the tide was low so that it could float off when the tide returned - thus allowing loading to continue when the sea level was too low.

You may find some of the aforementioned climbers exercising their limbs on the cliff face behind you whilst children play and people picnic. It's a very popular spot considering it isn't the easiest place in the world to get to - with a reasonable walk and a steep climb either before you arrive or when you leave. This is where you may find groups of young men (and, rarely, girls) jumping from ridiculous heights into the deep blue sea where small boats were once loaded with quarried stone to be taken out to London-bound ships which were anchored safely away from the dangerous cliffs.

After your visit to Dancing Ledge, turn West through the stone wall and pass the stone marked 'Coast Path. Seacombe 1'. The whole Coast Path undulates endlessly and I will not be constantly referring to 'up' and 'down' as you go. However, follow the fence on the sloping grass with the downs up on your right and with views ahead to more cliff quarries and the outstanding strip lynchets on East and West Man.

As you leave 'Spyway Farm Estate' over a stile with two steps on the other side, drop down to a long bridge which will be useful when the 'Eastington' stream decides to flood the grass here. On the other side, the path makes a left turn as a wide grass track heads away along the Eastington valley. You are skirting around the top of two cliff quarries with more loading ledges below you. These are very minor works and are overshadowed by their neighbours, Seacombe and Winspit.

Keep going, passing a stile which leads onto the cliff top and cross a hollow by any one choice of its innumerable paths. Walk up to the stile and climb over.

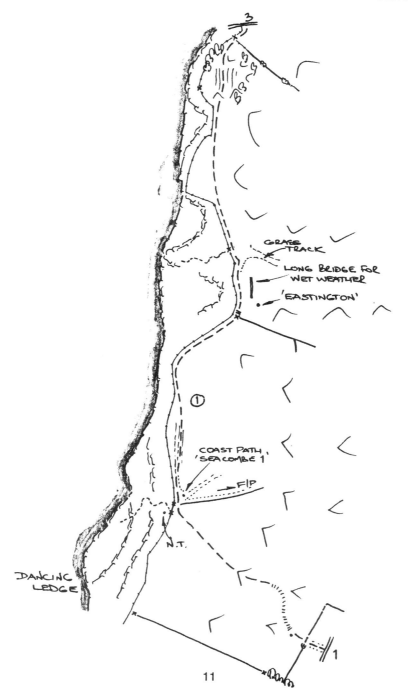

ROUTE 1 - STAGE 3

EASTINGTON TO SEACOMBE

Still enjoying the lovely, breezy coastal walk with the waves foaming up against the cliffs, the strip lynchets above Winspit are coming ever closer. Soon, the undulating path arrives at another stile which overlooks the cliffs, scattered debris and platforms of Seacombe Quarry. Over the stile, the path bears right and descends quite steeply to cross a plank/sleeper bridge over a wet weather stream which emanates from the Eastington valley on the right.

At the foot of the slope, a stone marker points back to 'Dancing Ledge 1'. There is a stile next to the gate which leads a limestone rubble track into the closed quarry on your left. You can go over to explore if you wish. It is certainly a good spot for a coffee stop or a lunch break with many large stone blocks being happy to act as al fresco benches.

In the 1920s, The Dorset Quarry Co used open-cast methods and tunnels to extract large blocks of Purbeck and Portland stone from this quarry. Unlike Dancing Ledge, most of the stone was raised to the top of the quarry by steam-driven cranes and transported by horse wagons up the valley to Eastington. With the rise of Swanage as a stone port, the loads then travelled from there to Langton Matravers and Swanage.

Leaving Seacombe Quarry over the same stile, follow the track up the valley, away from the sea for about 50 yards. Turn left off the track where a stone marker advises that it is 1 mile to Worth Matravers along the valley and 3/4 mile to Winspit. A sign 'Old Quarry Workings...' advises of the dangers of exploring unstable areas as you reach the foot of a flight of Purbeck stone steps. With bushes on either side, go up the steps and emerge onto the cliff path at the top.

Ignore the stile and Footpath arrow on your right but keep following the Coast Path to the next stile. The strip lynchets of East Man are now on your right as you follow a levelled section which was once part of the second access road to the top of Seacombe Quarry. Follow the fence to a stile with a 'Coast Path' stone and climb over to pass an old wooden seat on your left and a deep, almost circular quarry on your right. The path narrows at the quarry and leads into a bushy, brambly area.

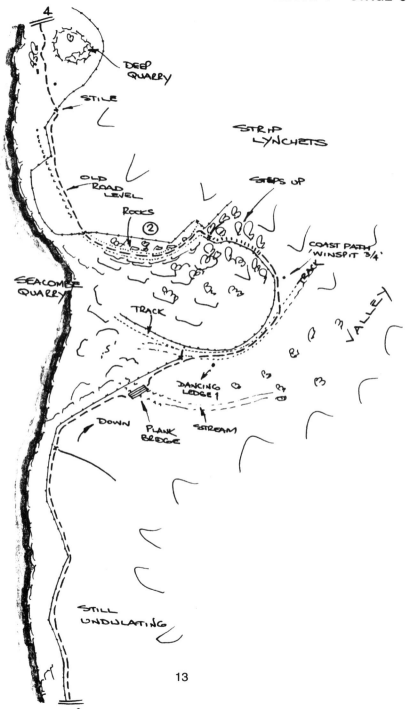

4

DEEP QUARRY

STILE

STRIP LYNCHETS

OLD ROAD LEVEL

STEPS UP

ROCKS

②

COAST PATH /WINSPIT 3/4'

SEACOMBE QUARRY

TRACK

TRACK

VALLEY

DANCING LEDGE 1

DOWN

PLANK BRIDGE

STREAM

STILL UNDULATING

13

2

ROUTE 1 - STAGE 4

WINSPIT TO WORTH MATRAVERS

After the 'Eastington' sign, go through a gap in the bushes and past a stile in the fence on your right.   Actually, this stile will probably come into more use as the cliff path erodes further.   If you were to go over it now and follow the other side of the fence, you would be following the new path to Winspit.   If you feel like a trail-blazer - who would like to keep away from the cliff edge - go that way now.

For now, the cliff path keeps close to the cliff side of the wire fence and, in a few yards, the path is quite close to the edge.   Keep on to another stile where you have a second chance to go over onto the safer side before you fall into Winspit Quarry.   Either way, the path bears right with fine views into the workings below you.   Turning inwards, join the narrow path and begin to descend the path and steps into a bush-filled area which fills the stream valley from Worth Matravers down into Winspit.   The grass track which runs inland from the top stile would lead you into Worth without going down into the quarry if you want to take it.

Arriving at a limestone rubble terrace, a faint path on your left leads to one of two tunnels which have been sealed off with steel cages to let bats nest in them undisturbed - so resolve not to bother going.   There's only the barrier to see and you might waken the bats.   Then a Coast Path marker tells you that it's 1.1/4 miles to Worth.

Feel free to wander around the workings.   Not only are they bigger but they're more popular than Seacombe because they're more easily accessible.   There are remnants of the actual quarry sheds and bases of the cranes which tore the immense stone blocks out of the quarry face after they had been freed.

The rising track which runs from Winspit to Worth Matravers is the very same route along which teams of 16 horses struggled to pull the heavy loads of stone ready for onward shipment from the village to the port of Ower in the present Poole Harbour.   Although most cliff quarries used nothing but seaward shipping, they were restricted by weather.   Winspit gained by having a gradual, if arduous, route up to the quarry village of Worth.   The later expansion of Swanage into a stone shipping port brought welcome relief to Winspit as the route from Worth to Swanage was far easier than that to the little port below Wareham.

Leaving Winspit, follow the rough track, past the 'Coast Path' which turns up the side of the quarry to 'St Aldhelm's Head' and past the second faint path to a bat cave.

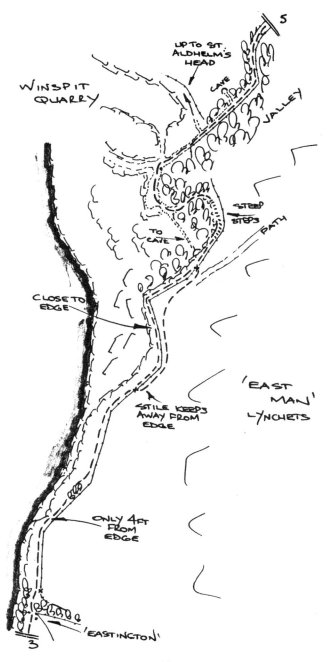

ROUTE 1 - STAGE 5

WINSPIT TO WORTH MATRAVERS

As you travel up this stony track, you have West Man on your left and East Man across the valley on your right. The little Winspit Bottom valley is rather densely filled with willows, sycamore, brambles, elderberries and, on your immediate right, escallonias with the small, bright green, shiny leaves and the little clusters of pink/red flowers.

There have been several references to lynchets since the walk started. These are simply areas of hillside divided into small fields by walls of turf or stone. Natural erosion, together with farming activities and ploughing with oxen, caused the higher ground within each field to migrate downwards. The walls stopped the soil from running straight down the hills and assisted the levelling process. Many of these lynchets date back to prehistoric times but the system is still used today. Over on West Man, you can sometimes see small areas of corn being grown just above Winspit itself. The naming of the downs, which reach out towards the sea, as 'East Man' and 'West Man' has, according to Langton Matravers historian Reg Saville, an anatomical origin which is best glossed over.

Anyway, you soon arrive at the driveway of Winspit Cottage on your right. Until the barn over on your left was recently converted, this was the only homestead so far down the valley. Go through the gate or over the stone stile and follow the shady track ever upwards. The track is soon less crowded by bushes and one of the alternative Footpath branches from above Winspit comes back over the stile on your right. Just here, the track bears left to 'Renscombe 1' and to take vehicles up to the village road. Turn off onto the path which goes straight on to 'Worth 1/2', alongside the wire fence round a small water treatment plant. Go over the next stile into the more open head of the Winspit Bottom valley.

A faint path follows the lower level but bear slightly left and follow the uphill path, diagonally towards Worth Matravers. Near the top, go over another stile in the hedge into an enclosed path which leads to the last stile before the village. This brings you out onto a tarmac lane in front of a row of old stone cottages called 'London Row'.

Now is the time to be considering whether to indulge yourself with an ice-cream or a full Dorset cream tea at the tea shop or, if you are within the old licensing hours, a little liquid refreshment at the most perfect of Purbeck pubs, the 'Square and Compass'. Actually, one cold and windy January morning on the Priests Way near Acton, I met a charming lady on horseback who, it turned out, runs the tea shop in Worth. Having enjoyed several teas and ice-creams over the years, I said I would point my fellow walkers in her direction. So I have. Go for it!

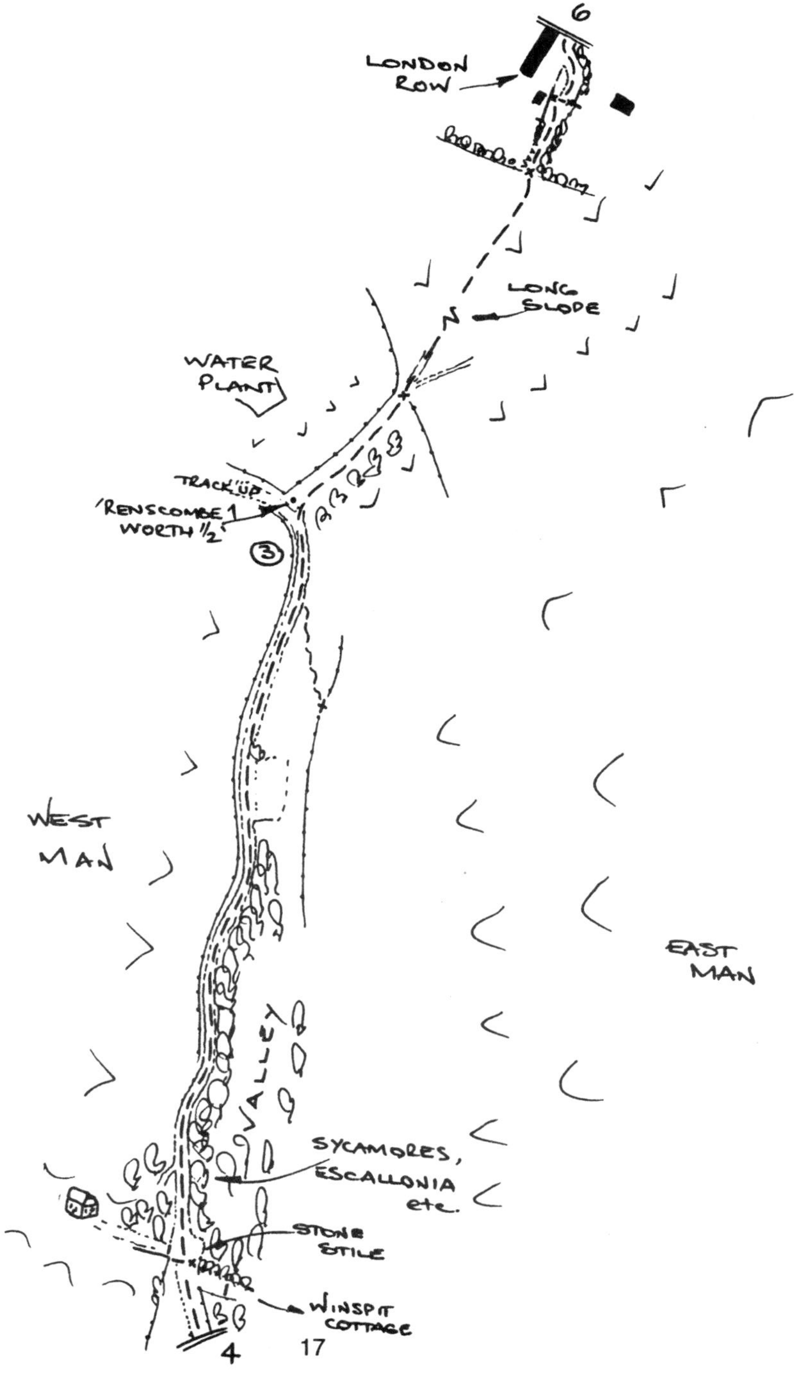

6

LONDON ROW

LONG SLODE

N

WATER PLANT

TRACK UP

RENSCOMBE 1
WORTH ½

③

WEST MAN

VALLEY

EAST MAN

SYCAMORES,
ESCALLONIA
etc.

STONE STILE

WINSPIT COTTAGE

4   17

ROUTE 1 - STAGE 6

WORTH MATRAVERS TO ABBASCOMBE FARM

As you leave 'London Row', the village green and duck pond are over the road and, as you bear right around its edge, you pass the bus shelter and telephone box on your left.

On the RH corner, there is a signpost for 'Winspit 1. Seacombe 1. Durlston 4.1/4'. Of more immediate interest, as you continue around the edge of the green, the tea rooms are on your left, beyond the duck pond.

Also worth a visit is St Nicholas' Parish Church. St Nicholas is the patron saint of sailors and the lovely stone church with stone slate roof stands high up behind a row of fine lime trees. This was once the parish which held the tiny fishing village of Swanage within its boundary. Worth Matravers' rectors used to walk from here along the downland path to Swanage to take services. But this was hundreds of years ago. By the late 15thC, Swanage was already the more important of the two villages and the rector lived there and walked to Worth instead. The path still exists. It is the 'Priests' Way' which we will be following when we leave Worth.

There is a squint built into the South wall of St Nicholas' so that villagers who were stricken with the plague during the Black Death of 1348-49 could see the altar and the service within.

Benjamin Jesty was buried here in 1816. He is the farmer from Yetminster in North Dorset who discovered the qualities of the common cowpox as a protection against the deadly smallpox. Being already immune himself, he inoculated his wife and sons with cowpox to prove his theory. He later sold his Upbury Farm and moved here to Worth.

Further along the road, you reach a junction where you go straight on past the turning to the Craft Centre on your right and a track up to the 'Square and Compass' on your left. There is a useful W.C. in the car park up the road on your left past a side entrance to the 'Square and Compass'. I think that is every bodily comfort sorted out now so, leaving Worth, gastronomically, physically and spiritually refreshed, walk on along the same road.

There are various houses on your left and the head of the Winspit Bottom valley is on your right. Keep on past a bus stop and a stile into the field before some stone houses on your right. After Newfoundland Close, you reach a large barn in a yard over the stone wall, also on your left.

Immediately, go over the stile in the RH wire fence, signposted for 'Swanage 4'. Bear left across the corner of the field to find another stile in the fence where a concrete drive runs across your path from the road to Abbascombe Farm. Go over the next stile, signed 'Purbeck Heritage' on its other side.

Cross this next field on a grassy path towards another stile in the stone wall, almost in the far RH corner. Over this stile, take a long look across the next field and aim for the fingerpost in the distance on the other side.

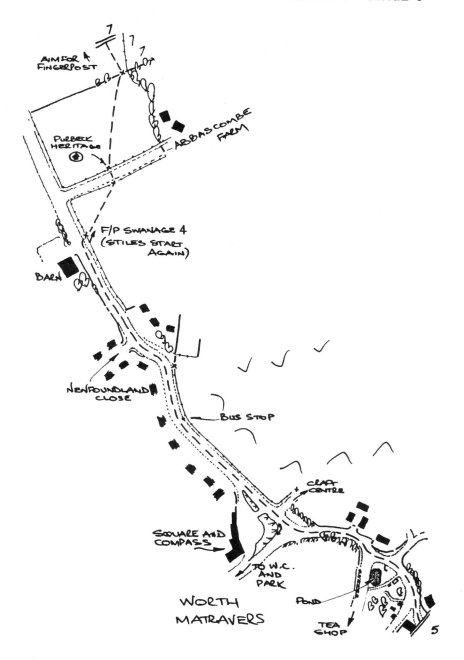

AIM FOR A
FINGERPOST

PURBECK
HERITAGE

ABBASCOMBE
FARM

F/P SWANAGE 4
(STILES START
AGAIN)

BARN

NEWFOUNDLAND
CLOSE

BUS STOP

CRAFT
CENTRE

SQUARE AND
COMPASS

TO W.C.
AND
PARK

POND

WORTH
MATRAVERS

TEA
SHOP

5

ABBASCOMBE FARM TO DURNFORD DROVE

Crossing this field, there are good views across the head of the Eastington valley to the sea on your right.   Arriving at the fingerpost, go through the half-gate onto a gravel track which runs between distant stone walls.   You are now firmly on 'Priests' Way' and following in the footsteps of hundreds of years of clerics and many thousands of cattle being moved from village to village or field to field.

The stone marker advises that you have already come 3/4 mile from Worth so there isn't much further to go today.   That's a shame.   This has been a super walk.   However, a crossing with cattle grids on opposite branches, takes you past Eastington Farm on your right and your level stroll continues along Priests' Way.

200 yards later, there are stiles to either side, the left leading to the top road and the right to 'Seacombe 1'.   Keep straight on and, after a while, go over another stile next to a gate across your path and keep going again until you reach some quarry workings on your left.

This is Acton.   The whole village has been undermined over the years and the crust is mostly no more than 15ft thick below the cottages.   The stone won from the area of this little hamlet comes from quite a narrow seam so the workings tend to be on a smaller scale.   When a patch is cleared of usable stone, the workings are filled in and moved a little further on.   Therefore, as time passes, quarrying operations will move around the Priests' Way area and the layout will vary from that suggested here.

Just in case the walls alongside the Priests' Way have not changed, I'll just tell you to do what I have done.   Go over two more stiles next to gates across the track and past a couple of stone cottages on your left.   Soon, there are fine views over the left wall towards the Isle of Wight and Ballard Down again.   Then there are stiles to left and right with signs for 'Langton 3/4. Swanage 2.1/4' and 'Coast Path Hedbury' respectively.

About 1/4 mile on, there is a good view of Langton Matravers itself and then a stile on your right leads onto the inland path which you saw as you left 'Dancing Ledge'.   Opposite this stile, another one is signed for 'Langton 1/2 and Toms Field'.

Keep straight on, through another gate and stile and, before you know it, you'll be back at the cross tracks where you first met Spyway Farm.   Turn left onto the return track and follow the grassy edge of the track back to the kissing gate, your car or Durnford Drove into Langton Matravers.   What a lovely walk.

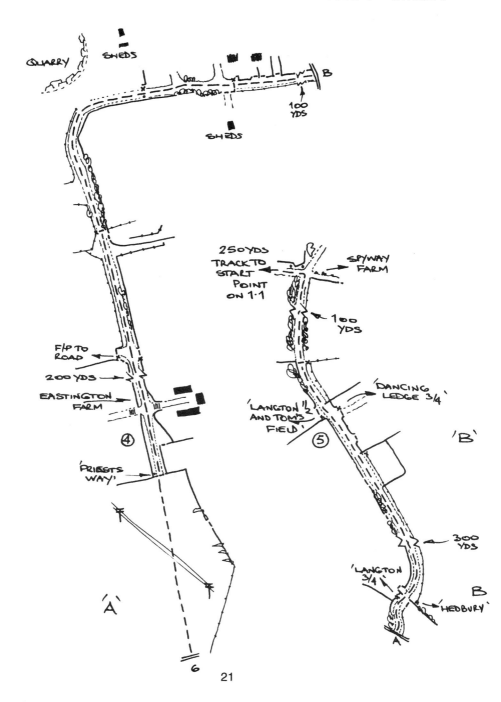

QUARRY

SHEDS

B

100
YDS

SHEDS

250YDS
TRACK TO
START
POINT
ON 1·1

SPYWAY
FARM

100
YDS

F/P TO
ROAD

200 YDS

EASTINGTON
FARM

DANCING
LEDGE 3/4

'LANGTON 1/2
AND TOMS
FIELD'

④

⑤

'B'

'PRIESTS
WAY'

300
YDS

'LANGTON
3/4'

B

'A'

'HEDBURY'

A

6

21

ROUTE 2 - STAGE 1

ACTON CAR PARK TO HAYCRAFT LANE

Leaving the car park, cross the B3069 and climb over the Footpath-arrowed stile in the stone wall between the bus stop and the telephone box.   Bear slightly right and walk across the field to a hawthorn-hedged bank on the far RH side.   There, with a stone shed lurking in the corner, go up the bank and climb over the unsigned stile.   In this next field, cross over the track and aim for the stile in the far RH corner again.   This one has a Footpath arrow on it.

On the other side, follow the grass path between a LH low stone wall and a garden hedge on your right.   There are a couple of old barns over on your left.   Join the stony track that runs in front of a row of cottages but, where the track widens before it turns right to the road, go over the unsigned stile in the left fence.

Your route across this next long field passes about 30 yards to the right of the stone wall corner ahead of you and, on the way, brings you back slightly towards the earlier barns.   For those with compasses, the line is 310º NW.   On the far side, you will find a stile and stone steps over the wall in the corner next to Langton West Woods.   There is no arrow but, if you aim left of Corfe Castle in the distance (302º WNW), you will find the next stile in the wire fence on the far side of this open field.   Over the stile, cross the next field with good views of Nine Barrow Down far beyond the long house at the bottom of your field.

There are some large, grass covered water tanks up on your left.   I don't know why they have doors in them.   Why doesn't the water leak through the cracks in the doors?   Answers on a £5 note to the author, please.   Anyway, go over the two stiles in the thick hedge and keep straight on, passing the wire fenced wood on your right and the fenced house on the left with Scots pines on its borders.

Much of the track around here is paved with old Purbeck stone slabs such as are used for roofing.   The stone path is on a direct line from the Purbeck quarries to Dunshay Manor and from thence to Corfe Castle, becoming the railway line for the last 1.1/2 miles.   Perhaps the flagstones are the remnant of a road built to transport the stone to Downshay or beyond or perhaps it was a luxurious path from Langton Matravers to Corfe.   Downshay is of particular importance but there will be more about that when you get closer.   It seems that every time you go out for a walk, you come back with a little more knowledge but a lot more questions.

Go over the stile into Haycraft Lane with a signpost pointing back for 'Footpath Langton 1'.   Turn right and walk past the Bridleway for 'Wilkswood' on your right and down the banked, hedged lane.   Rising again, go past the left turns for Downshay Farm and Dunshay Manor.   A few yards further, go over the Footpath arrowed stile with a fingerpost to 'Woody Hyde 3/4'.   There are more flagstones around this stile.   Cross the field to the next clearly visible stile.

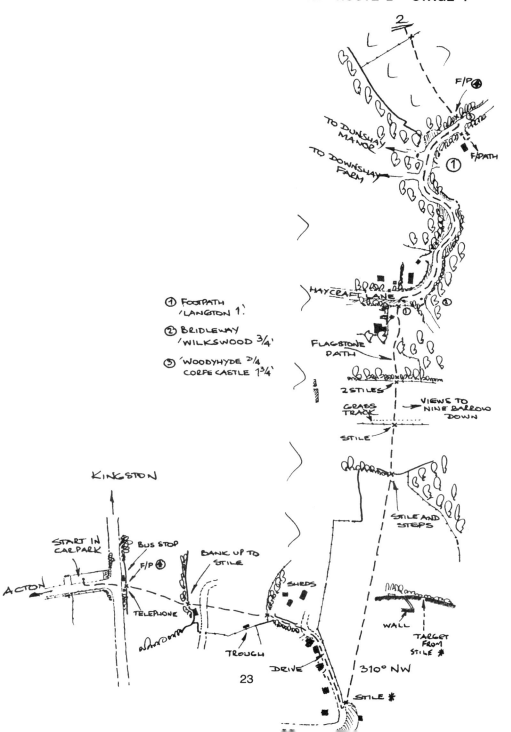

① FOOTPATH
/LANGTON 1'

② BRIDLEWAY
/WILKSWOOD 3/4'

③ 'WOODYHYDE 2/4'
CORFE CASTLE 1 3/4'

23

ROUTE 2 - STAGE 2

HAYCRAFT LANE TO WOODYHYDE FARM

Keep straight on to a stile in the high hedge.   *On the way across, you can see the vast tower of Kingston church away ahead of you, slightly left.   Somewhere beyond the hedges and in the trees on your left are Downshay Farm and Dunshay Manor.   The Manor House was built in the 1642 where once stood the medieval seat of the Matravers family who gave their name to Lytchett Matravers, Worth Matravers and Langton Matravers.   Downshay Farm is quite modern but has two 17thC stone-mullioned windows built into it.*

Take care at this stile.   The next field is particularly long and the way out of it is about 500 yards away.   Take a line along the top LH hedge and begin to walk along it but veering away from it gradually.   The track, signal box and platforms of Swanage Railway's Harman's Cross Station are all down on your right as you go.   By the time you reach the hedge at the far end, you should be about 60 yards away from the left hedge.   Here, you will find a wicket gate.

Through the gate, keep to your existing line, getting closer to the railway lines. Nearing the far side of this 400 yards long field, cross a ditch which runs from the hedge into your open field and you will find your next stile in an overgrown clump about 50 yards from the rail fence.   There is a willow tree standing in the stream on the other side.   This is Woodyhyde Camping Field.   Keep close to the LH hedge and walk straight on to the gravel track with the office hut and a telephone box on your right.   Turn right and follow the track under the railway bridge.

Now, just keep walking along the track, entrained between fences through two fields, past Woodyhyde Farm and its barns and up between two more fields.

17thC Westwood Farm - Page 28

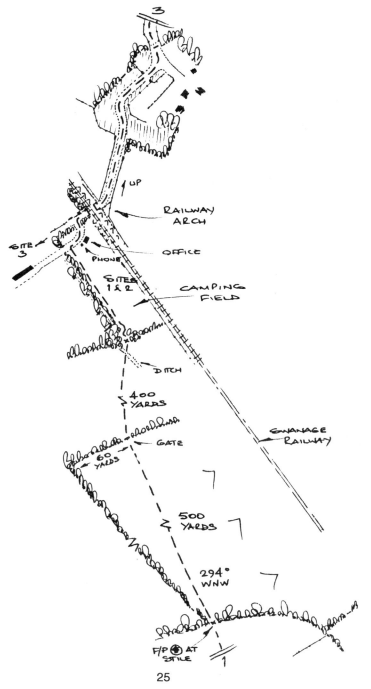

ROUTE 2 - STAGE 3

WOODYHYDE FARM TO LITTLE WOOLGARSTON

Soon you arrive at the A351 Swanage road. Here, a fingerpost points behind you to 'Bridleway Worth 2' - not a word about our path from Haycraft Lane.

Carefully now - this is the main road to Swanage - cross over and go through the half-gate onto the track across the field, signed 'Bridleway L. Woolgarston 1/2'. As you go, the railway line heading into Corfe Castle on your left would make a very good photograph.   About half-way across, the field descends quite steeply to a gate in the deep bottom hedge with a stream on the other side.   Through the gate, bear right and cross the corner of the field to follow the RH hedge and coppice up the rising field.   There will be a ditch inside the deep hedge as you progress up to a gate in the top RH corner of this field.

Cross the next field, aiming for two poles on either side of a gate in the far hedge. On arrival at this gate, a Bridleway arrow directs you straight on past rows of cattle sheds and outbuildings until you come to the far RH corner of the yard. Here, go through the unsigned gate onto the lane which runs through Little Woolgarston.   Immediately, a sign on your left points to Corfe Castle and A351.

Ignore it and keep straight on, along the lane until you have just passed Little Woolgarston Cottage on your right.   A fingerpost for 'Footpath Woolgarston 3/4' points down two steps into a hedged, ditched area with a sleeper bridge leading to a stile.   Arrows confirm this is the Footpath as you climb over into a fern-lined path between the LH field and the RH garden.

A little bridge crosses a small ditch and then you zig-zag past Footpath arrows to another sleeper bridge across another ditch which is awash with lush ferns. Over the stile, bear slightly left as you begin to climb the steep grassy field. Over the brow, note the gate in the left hedge but keep going until you see a stile in the top left corner.   You will be aiming straight towards Nine Barrow Down.   In the corner, you will see that there are two stiles with a Footpath arrow, next to another gate.   Go over the stiles and walk down the sloping field towards the stable in the adjacent field.

At the far end of the stable, there are two stiles to the left of the single large tree. Unfortunately, there are no arrows so bear half left and walk up the hill.

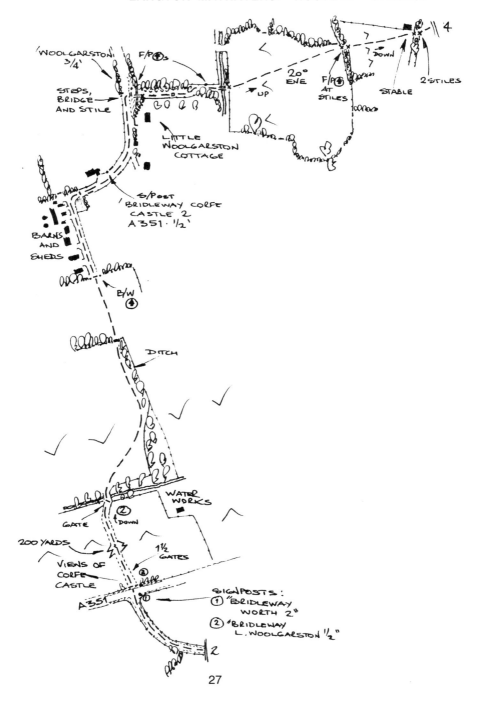

'WOOLGARSTON
3/4'

F/P ③

STEPS,
BRIDGE
AND STILE

20°
ENE

F/P ⑤
AT
STILES

DOWN

UP

2 STILES

STABLE

LITTLE
WOOLGARSTON
COTTAGE

S/POST
'BRIDLEWAY CORFE
CASTLE 2
A351 · 1/2'

BARNS
AND
SHEDS

B/W
④

DITCH

WATER
WORKS

②

GATE   DOWN

200 YARDS

VIEWS OF
CORFE
CASTLE

1½
GATES

④

A351   ①

SIGNPOSTS:
① 'BRIDLEWAY
    WORTH 2"
② 'BRIDLEWAY
    L. WOOLGARSTON 1/2"

2

27

LITTLE WOOLGARSTON TO WESTWOOD FARM

As you climb up the hill, you will can see a stile and gate with a fingerpost inside the field.   On arrival, the sign points back to 'Footpath L. Woolgarston 1/2'.   Go over the stile and into the sunken tarmac lane outside.   Turn right and walk down the lane.

Around the bend after the cottage on the left, turn down the lane to 'Woolgarston Farm' and walk quietly past the farmhouse, Willow Cottage and an old, square grain store, all on your left.   At some barns, the track goes through a Footpath-arrowed gate and passes an open area on the left before plunging down into a sunken, hedged track.   Don't go down the track.   A Footpath arrow points into the field to the left of the track.   Go through and follow the track's hedge, across a ditch and up to a Footpath-arrowed stile in the corner of a wire-fenced field.

Over the stile, walk straight up the field, regardless of where the arrow points, skirting around some bushes in the ditch as you go (145º SSE).   There is a gateway exit by a small tree in the top hedge with a Footpath arrow on the reverse side.   Through this gap, keep straight on to the right one of two openings in the facing hedge.   Through this opening, there will be a hedge on your left.   Veer sharply away from this hedge, ignoring any gates in the far end hedge, aiming for the far RH corner of the field where you will find twin stiles astride a deep hedge. There are fine views to the Swanage coast from here.

A Footpath arrow turns you sharp right, past a couple of trees, to a top gate.   Go through the gate and follow the LH wire fence closely down to the bottom of the hill.   Strange as it may seem, go through the bottom gate into the cattle pens and out the other side onto the road.   Here, a fingerpost points back to 'Footpath Woolgarston 1/2', but not back up the hill down which you just arrived.

Turn right and walk past several cottages and barns to a T-junction which is signposted for 'Westwood Farm' and 'Footpath New Buildings 3/4'.   Turn left and follow the bending lane to a gate into the farmyard.   Bear slightly right to pass Westwood farmhouse.   *The superb stone-mullioned Westwood Farm house was built in the early 17thC and the front is clearly unchanged.   There is a through-passage running through the house to the right of the left end window.*   Turn round the right end of the house and keep straight on to the farm gate into a high field.   Walk across the field, slightly to your left to another gate in the facing hedge.   Keep to the left of an electricity pole as you go.   At the gate, there is no indication of the direction of the Footpath and the far hedge cannot be seen over the brow of the hill.   So, bear slightly left (130º SE) and walk up and over the top.

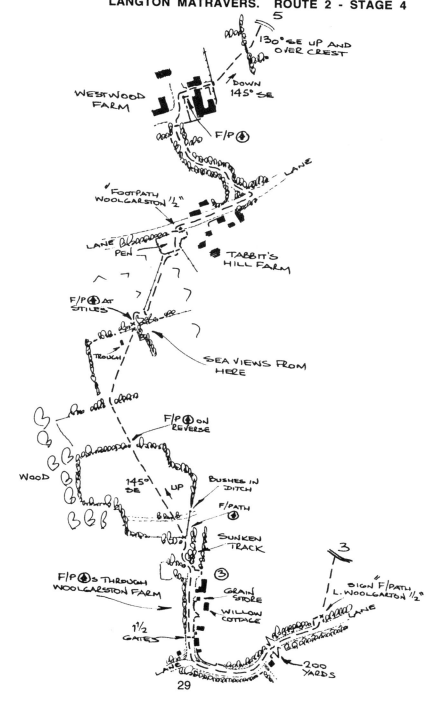

5

130° SE UP AND
OVER CREST

DOWN
145° SE

WESTWOOD
FARM

F/P ⊕

LANE

FOOTPATH
WOOLGARSTON ½"

LANE
PEN

TABBIT'S
HILL FARM

F/P ⊕ AT
STILES

TROUGH

SEA VIEWS FROM
HERE

F/P ⊕ ON
REVERSE

WOOD

145°
SE

UP

BUSHES IN
DITCH

F/PATH
⊕

BRAB

SUNKEN
TRACK

3

F/P ⊕s THROUGH
WOOLGARSTON FARM

③

SIGN "F/PATH
L. WOOLGARTON ½"

GRAIN
STORE

WILLOW
COTTAGE

LANE

1½
GATES

LANE

200
YARDS

29

ROUTE 2 - STAGE 5

WESTWOOD FARM TO WILKSWOOD

When you can see the far hedge down below you, maintain this direction and you will find the exit stile in the deep hedge.   If you don't find it first time, it's much nearer the left end than the right.

Over the un-arrowed stile, cross the ditch and keep going in exactly the same direction (half-left away from the stile).   Over the brow of this field, look back and you will see Westwood Farm on the exact 130º line which you followed to get here.   In the bottom corner of this field, go over the stile with a Footpath arrow on the reverse.   Walk up the next field with an orchard on your right, aiming due South to a spot 40 yards left of the top RH corner.

Go over the stile by a sign for 'Ailwood 3/4 and Woolgarston 1' onto the verge of the A351.   This is a bit near a bend on your right so walk down the verge to your left until you're sure it's safe to cross over to the pavement on the other side. Then, turn down the tarmac drive signed for 'Quarr Farm 1/2 and Haycrafts 3/4'. You have now completed a whole circuit of the village of Harman's Cross without having had more than a glimpse of its mostly modern houses.   Walk down the entrained track to the level crossing over the Swanage Railway track. Remember, "Stop. Look. Listen".

Safely across, walk up the farm track and past the left turn which goes to Quarr Farm itself.   Keeping to the low track, follow it around a left bend and uphill past a spring-fed pond with trees on the left.   Arriving in the barn-filled yards, keep straight on past the stone gable end of a 17thC barn and, whatever the state of gates (open, closed, there or not), turn left at a Bridleway arrow and walk between stables, Quarr House and a long barn.   Go through the gate at the end and keep straight on, past a World War II hut straight out of a Biggles movie.   Ignore the Bridleway, Footpath and Permissive Path arrows on your right and keep straight on through one last gate into a wood.

Inside the wood, there are plaques for 'Wilkswood' and 'National Trust'.   Keep to the main track as it meanders, rises and falls through coppiced hazels and old trees.   When the track passes through gateposts in a wire fence, look out for a right Footpath turning in about 100 yards.   Three arrows confirm directions of the Bridleway which you are leaving and the Footpath which you are joining.   Follow the Footpath steps down through gorse and bracken into a coppiced wood. Cross a stone slab bridge over a stream at the bottom with a fern gully on your left and scattered rocks all over the place.

Bear left and follow the sunken, rocky path up through the scrub and out into an area resembling an ancient common.   There is bracken, gorse, scrub and hawthorn all around.   Cross over a grass track and walk left of an electricity pole with an arrow on it.   Rising now, follow the vague grass path straight on through thickets until it bears slightly right in its ascent into more open grassland.   Climb over the Footpath-arrowed stile in the wire fence at the top.

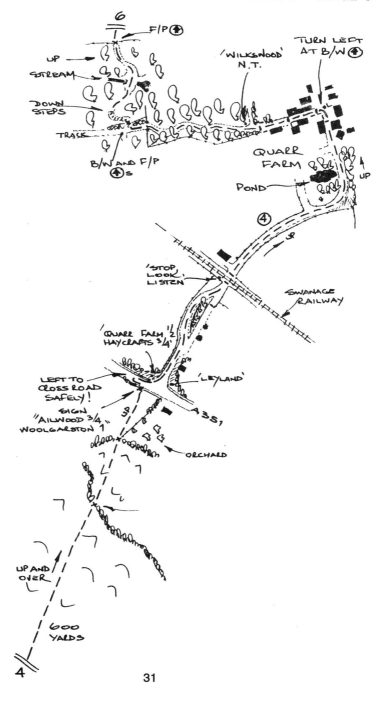

ROUTE 2 - STAGE 6

WILKSWOOD TO ACTON CAR PARK

Walk up through the scrub to the top stile.　　Over this stile, bear slightly left so that you meet the hedge about 100 yards up on your left (160º SSE).

Go over the stile by the farm gate and turn sharp right along the hedge.　　At the top, go through a Footpath-arrowed kissing gate near the RH corner.　　Cross this next, rising field, aiming for the top left corner and admiring the views towards the sea on your left.　　Go through the top gate and cross the small yard to the opposite gate with Scots pines in the far bank.　　Through this gate, turn sharp right and instantly left to follow the farm track away from the cluster of barns. There will be sports fields on your left belonging to Old Malthouse School.

At the first crossing with three Footpath arrows and Durnford View on the RH corner, turn right and walk up to a Footpath-arrowed stile leading into a high field. Cross straight over the field and go over the next stile in a stone wall with trees standing along the far side.　　There is an angular stone house away across the field in front of you.　　Aim well to the left of it and, as you traverse this next longer field, veer even further left.　　Your new target is the far end of the low stone cottage with the roadside wall running between itself and the first 'target' house.

When you reach the road wall, go over the stile onto the roadside pavement.　　A fingerpost points back to 'Haycrafts 3/4' and a plaque confirms 'N.T. Wilkswood'. Turn right and follow the pavement to the drive to the stone house which turns out to be 'Castle View'.　　Instantly cross over the road into the gate, fence and stile collection on the other side.　　Don't go over the stile.　　Go through the gate and follow the raised grass track at first, veering away from the fence and aiming for the RH end of the first stone house in the cluster of cottages that are Acton.

The bumps and hollows that have you stumbling up and down on the way are the remains of years and years of near-surface quarrying - and this area is one of the major sources of the famous Purbeck marble.　　At the end of the stone house, go over the stile and turn right onto the tarmac lane.　　Follow the lane back to the car park where you started this intriguing walk.

Acton viewed from Tom's Field, Langton Matravers

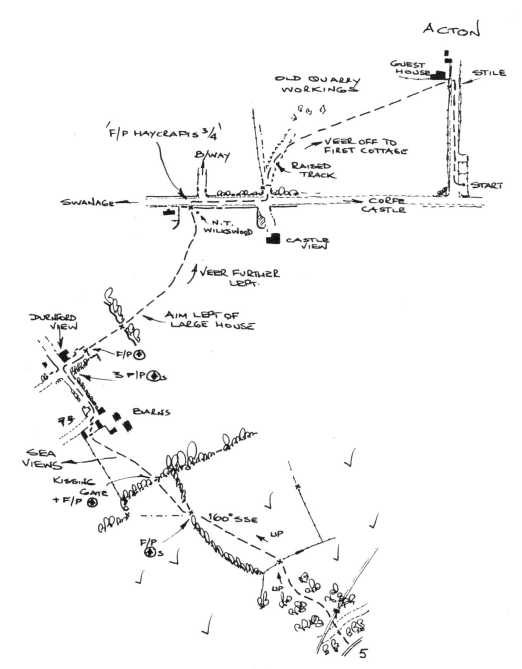

ACTON

GUEST HOUSE

STILE

OLD QUARRY WORKINGS

'F/P HAYCRAFTS ¾'

B/WAY

VEER OFF TO FIRST COTTAGE

RAISED TRACK

START

SWANAGE

CORFE CASTLE

N.T. WILKSWOOD

CASTLE VIEW

VEER FURTHER LEFT.

DURNFORD VIEW

AIM LEFT OF LARGE HOUSE

F/P

3 F/Ps

BARNS

SEA VIEWS

KISSING GATE + F/P

160° SSE

UP

F/Ps

UP

5

33

PART 2 - STURMINSTER NEWTON

INTRODUCTION

I have always welcomed any reason for returning to the 'capital' of the Blackmore Vale and, whilst working on the 'Stour Valley Way' venture with Dorset County Council, I found myself wanting to wander off again to enjoy the country walking around Manston.   The 'Stour Valley Way' long-distance trail passes Hammoon and Fiddleford Mill but the two walks in this section take you on lovely circular ambles - on more or less level ground for a change - to see some of the lovely countryside that the long-distance path has to miss.   Some of the Manston paths were used in 'Rambles from Dorset Towns' but, this time, the longer circuit includes Hammoon with its superb thatched manor house and its lovely little church, St Paul's.   The walks also visit Sturminster Mill and Fiddleford Mill which has a beautiful mill pond on the River Stour and (I quote) "the most spectacular Timber roof in Dorset".

These are particularly lovely strolls with many surprises and much to delight the naturalist and the amateur historian.

THE ALTERNATIVES

Both walks begin and end in Sturminster Newton's Market Square - at Reference ST787142 on O S Map No. 194

Parking is easy with a large free car park just off the town centre whilst there are many buses routes.   First Southern National 68 and X94 are supplemented by hosts of routes by Damory Coaches - far too many to list here.

ROUTE 1: Total distance 6.3/4 miles - This walk begins in Sturminster Newton and, after a wander past Sturminster Mill and the site of the iron age hill fort at 'New Town', it goes off on field paths to Broad Oak before leading you through lovely Piddles Wood.   After Fiddleford, the circuit follows the old rail track and field paths to Hammoon for a visit to the lovely little church of St Paul's.   Then, a short walk leads to Manston and a glimpse of a small mausoleum which has a unique place in the history of burial practice in England.   An easy amble through long riverside fields, leads back to Sturminster for a final stroll with William Barnes connections.

ROUTE 2: Total distance 3.1/2 miles - This Route is the same as Route 1 through Broad Oak and Piddles Wood but it permits a quick return from Fiddleford Mill to Sturminster without visiting Hammoon or Manston.

STAGE	MILES	TOTAL MILES
ROUTE 1:		
1 Sturminster Newton to Hole House Lane	1.5	1.5
2 Hole House Lane to Piddles Wood	.75	2.25

STAGE	MILES	TOTAL MILES
3 Piddles Wood to Hammoon Fields	1.25	3.5
4 Hammoon Fields to Manston Meadows	1.25	4.75
5 Manston Meadows to Stour Path	1	5.75
6 Stour Path to Sturminster Newton	1	**6.75**

ROUTE 2:

STAGE	MILES	TOTAL MILES
1 Sturminster Newton to Hole House Lane	1.5	1.5
2 Hole House Lane to Piddles Wood	.75	2.25
3 Piddles Wood to Fiddleford Mill and riverside path to Sturminster Newton	1.25	3.5
6 Last leg into Sturminster Newton	.5	**4**

ROUTE LAYOUT

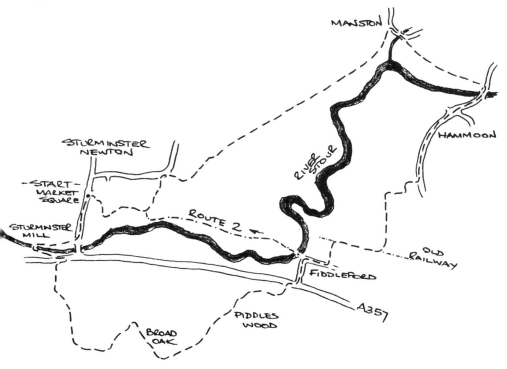

STAGE 1

STURMINSTER NEWTON TO HOLE HOUSE LANE

Standing in Market Square, with the 'Swan Inn' on your left, begin this superb walk by heading straight on along the narrowing road past Candy's Newsagents where you should stock up with a few chocolates before you get too far.   After Candy's, you pass the 15thC market cross and the thatched Town Council Office over on your left .

Walk down the main road, past Ricketts Lane and Church Lane and down the hill to cross Durrant with the first open field of the day on your right.   Keep on along the pavement, past the traffic lights, until you find a kissing gate and a footpath arrow pointing to 'Sturminster Mill 1/4'.   Go through the gate and drop down into the meadow alongside the River Stour.   A few yards out, you will have a fine view of the Town Bridge and its stone cutwaters.   *The bridge was built in the late 15thC-early 16thC and it was widened as long ago as the 17thC.*

Follow the fenced edge of the river all the way to a kissing gate with a signpost to 'Colber Bridge 1/2' pointing up the field to your right.   Go through the gate onto a path over the bridges and sluice gates of Sturminster Mill.   *This might be a good point to explain why this is called Sturminster Mill and not Sturminster Newton Mill.   There were originally four ancient settlements - Sturminster, Colber, Bagber and Newton.   The pre-conquest settlement to the South of the River Stour is listed in the Domesday Book as 'Newentone'.   Sturminster - or Stour Minster - lay on the North side and here are the Parish Church of St Mary and the mill.   Newton has neither a church nor a mill.   It does have a 'Castle' though - actually, the ruined manor house of the Manor of Newton which stands in the remains of an iron age fort's defences.   It was acquired by Glastonbury Abbey in 968AD but they lost it at the Dissolution and it fell into ruin.*

Leaving the mill, follow the driveway up to join the A357 Blandford to Sherborne road and turn left.   Cross the road at a convenient break in the traffic.   Opposite the Town Bridge, turn sharp right at the footpath sign for 'Hole House Lane 1/2' and walk up the narrow driveway past the 1870 Primitive Methodist Church and a house on your left.   At the top, go up the long flight of stone steps and over the stile into a high field with the stables and cottage of Castle Farm over on your right.   The remains of the 'Castle' are over the fence on your left.

Follow the left edge of this field and go over a stile mid-way along the next wire fence.   Cross the next field to a gate with a signpost outside.   This points back to 'Town Bridge 1/2' and on to 'Hole House lane 1/4'.   Keep straight on, keeping close to the woods on the left edge of the next curving, rising field.   In the top corner of this field, go over the stile or through the gate into a hedged hollow-way.

After 80 yards, and past Hole House low down on your left, you emerge onto a country lane.   On your immediate left, after Hole House's driveway, there is a signpost for 'Broad Oak 1/2' pointing down into a narrow, hedged path.   Go down this path for 100 yards and you will find a concrete and rail track footbridge over a little stream which is heading for the River Stour.   Over the bridge, follow the path round and up a flight of steps to a kissing gate into a long, rising field.   Keep straight on up the field, near the LH hedge.

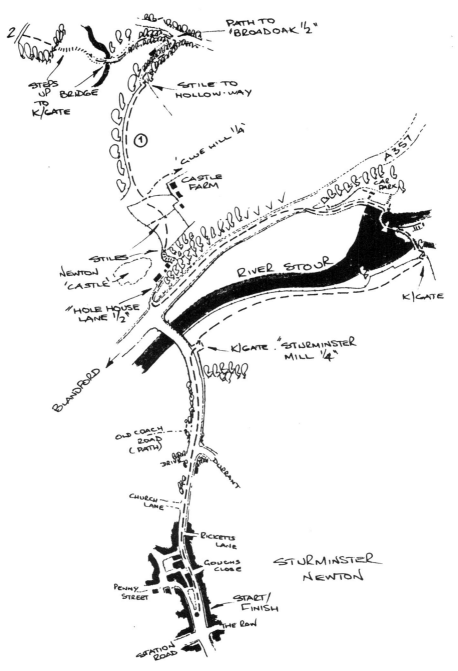

STAGE 2

HOLE HOUSE LANE TO PIDDLES WOOD

This field is 1/4 mile long but, as you progress, look back occasionally for lovely views to the Okeford Hill and Bulbarrow ridge, especially nearer the top end. Go through the footpath-arrowed kissing gate into a short track between houses.

This is Broad Oak and, at the road with a signpost back to 'Hole House Lane 1/2', turn left for a few paces before turning sharp right again, opposite a telephone box, into Copse Hill. Walk up the lane with a few houses on either side. When these are left behind, the verges widen out. There are now farm entrances and a scattering of barns behind both hedges.

In 1/4 mile, a footpath sign points through the farmyard on your right to 'Broad Oak 1/4'. Immediately after this, there is a car park on your left with a height gauge for 'Max Height 2m'. A signpost outside the entrance shows the way for 'A357 & Fiddleford Mill 1'. This is the way in to Piddles Wood. This fine mixed wood is owned by Hinton St Mary Estates and leased to the Dorset Wildlife Trust as a nature reserve. On your return, in preparation for a later visit, you can get a leaflet for the Nature Trail from the Stour Valley Rangers' office. For now, you have much further to go.

At first, the trees on your right are deciduous larches whilst the woods to your left include oaks, birches and holly. Some distance away to the right, you may sometimes hear the baying of several Hounds of the Baskervilles. I have not investigated the source of these sounds. In another 1/4 mile, a path meanders across your own track at a prominent sweet chestnut tree. Keep straight on along this high, wide ridge.

A little later, a footpath sign points onwards to 'A357, Fiddleford Mill 3/4' and off to the right to 'Angiers Farm'. Still keep straight on. Soon, you reach a huge oak tree at a clearing on your right. Here, the A357 path turns left and the right path goes to 'Angers Lane'. That's right. The farm is 'Angiers' but the road is Angers Lane. Keep straight on again as the path bears right and there are lovely glimpses towards the Rixon end of Sturminster Newton and to Duncliffe Hill. The traffic roar is coming up from the A357 just below.

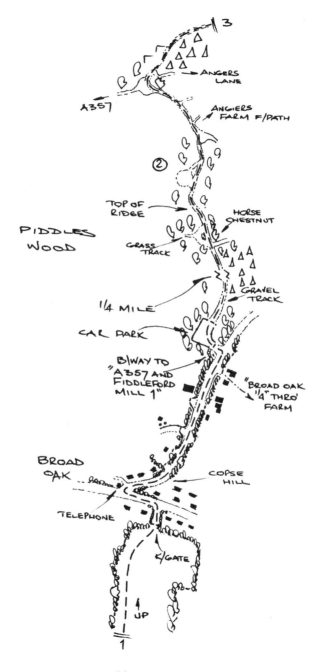

PIDDLES WOOD TO FIDDLEFORD AND HAMMOON FIELDS

In just another 50 yards, turn left at the Bridleway arrow and descend the winding path through the bracken and into a belt of trees to the very edge of the A357. Take great care as you peer out into the road looking for the lane that you need on the other side of the road.   It is a little down to your right.   When all is quiet, step out onto the road and hurry along on this side.   If something comes along, step onto the verge but try not to if at all possible as this, and the verge opposite, is dedicated as a 'Wildlife Verge'.

At the English Heritage 'Fiddleford Manor' sign, cross over the road and descend the lane between high hedges.   It is 300 yards to Fiddleford Manor and Mill car park on your left.   *The 14thC and 16thC roofs of the hall and solar of the Manor House are of national importance.   The trusses and windbraces are beautifully ornate and the designs are reproduced faithfully in the Royal Commission on Historic Monuments Volume for Dorset Central.*

After the car park, stop at the right turn in the lane.   The tarmac drive on your left leads to the Mill and the lane to your right continues your walk to Hammoon.   This is where you can go back to Sturminster Newton on Route 2 if you wish.

ROUTE 2: Go down the drive into Fiddleford Mill yard.   Follow the path round and over the sluice gates.   Cross the weir bridge and go through the kissing gate.   Follow the path straight on, not the one to 'Railway Path'.   Go over the stile in the hedge and the bridge across a ditch.   This leads into a very long field with the river on your left and a hedge on your right.   Follow the grass path, aiming for the gap in the far hedge 550 yards away.   Past the footpath arrow, follow the RH hedge.   Bear right at a huge oak tree and go over the stile into another field.   Turn half-left and walk to the left of two electricity poles.   Then turn to Stage 6 to join the Route 2 walkers for the last leg.

ROUTE 1: Turn right, over the bridge and follow the lane between the LH hedge and the RH wood until you reach the first left turning with a signpost to 'Hammoon 1.1/4'.   Turn up the long track, which sometimes harbours puddles long after the rain has gone away, and follow it between hedges for 1/4 mile.

When the old, banked railway track crosses your route, turn right at the Bridleway pointers.   Instantly, you can see Duncliffe Hill away on your left and Hambledon Hill just right of straight on.   As bushes allow, you will see Melbury Beacon half-left ahead of you and Okeford Hill to your right.   Your communing with old steam trains lasts for 1/2 mile in total before you find another Bridleway pointer.   Turn left and drop down the embankment to a gate into the narrow end of a long field.

Cross the corner and go over a small bridge over a stream to a half gate with a Bridleway arrow.   In the next long field, aim for the far RH corner.   *On the way, there are clearly visible remains of an ancient ridge and furrow cultivation system on your left.   The fields are in the parish of Hammoon.   They were enclosed before 1771 but the ridge and furrow system here dates back to medieval times.*

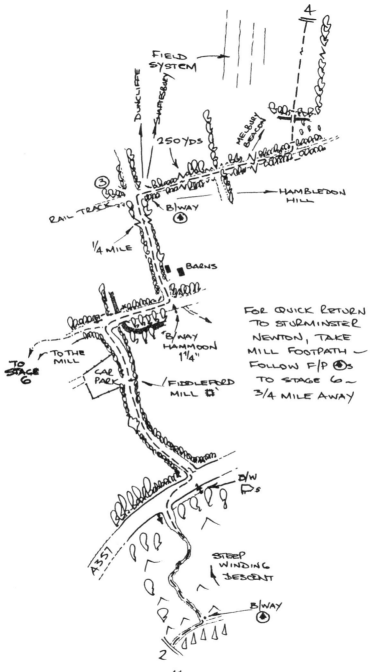

FIELD SYSTEM

DUNCLIFFE

SHAFTESBURY

250 YDS

MELBURY BEACON

③

RAIL TRACK ??

B/WAY

④

¼ MILE

HAMBLEDON HILL

BARNS

TO STAGE 6

TO THE MILL

B/WAY HAMMOON 1¼"

CAR PARK

FIDDLEFORD MILL #

FOR QUICK RETURN TO STURMINSTER NEWTON, TAKE MILL FOOTPATH ~ FOLLOW F/P ④s TO STAGE 6 ~ ¾ MILE AWAY

4

D/W P's

A357

STEEP WINDING DESCENT

B/WAY ④

2

STAGE 4

HAMMOON FIELDS TO MANSTON MEADOWS

Eventually arriving at the far end of the field, go through the farm gate onto a wide gravel track with a two-way Bridleway post outside.   Turn right and follow the track for 200 yards with Hambledon Hill straight ahead.   Keep on around a left and right bend and continue, with fine views of the ramparts of Hambledon Hill, to join the Hammoon road at a return-pointing Bridleway sign to 'Fiddleford 1.1/4'.

Turn left and walk 150 yards along the road (not very busy).   At the 'Hammoon' sign, another notice advises that there is 'No Footway for 600 yards'.   However, before long, you arrive in the little village with older houses on your left and newer ones on your right.   At the centre, where the base of the village cross remains on your left, turn left to a convenient bench outside the little church of St Paul's.

The church will repay a short visit.   As you go in through the heavy (probably 1400) South porch door and look down the nave, the first thing you will notice is that the chancel is offset to the left and the altar is out of line with the aisle.   It appears that the 13thC North aisle was demolished during the 15thC alterations and a new North wall built, leaving the chancel in this strange situation for the next 500 years at least.   At that same time, the floor level was raised.   In 1945, the chancel floor was lowered again to its original level and it is hoped that, before too long, the nave will be lowered as well.   The 15thC reredos and the 1959 East window are particularly interesting.   I must confess to wondering for a few moments who was the EMMA NUEL whose name appears, vertically divided, either side of the figure of Our Lord at the top of the window.

Back outside, a little further down the lane is the fine 16thC Manor House.   The lane is private, so keep your admiration of the fine stone walls and the unusual thatched roof on such a large house a distant one.

Leave this spot by walking up the road with Hammoon House behind the high wall and hedge on the RH corner.   Suddenly with open fields to left and right, follow the wooden fenced road for about 300 yards and cross the new bridge over the River Stour which was re-routed in 1966 to reduce flooding.   When the road becomes edged with trees on your left, go over the concrete stile in the iron fence, signposted ' Manston Church 1/2'.   Cross the footbridge and aim for the RH corner of the first field.   Go over the footpath-arrowed stile and a sleeper across the ditch in the next field.   Keep to the RH edge of this long, fenced field for about 500 yards.

Nearing the far end, if you look over to your left, you will see a small mausoleum in the trees.   This is in the grounds of Manston House and I'll tell you more about it on the next Stage.

Go over the end stile onto an enclosed farm track which runs parallel to the road on the other side of the hedge.   Turn left.

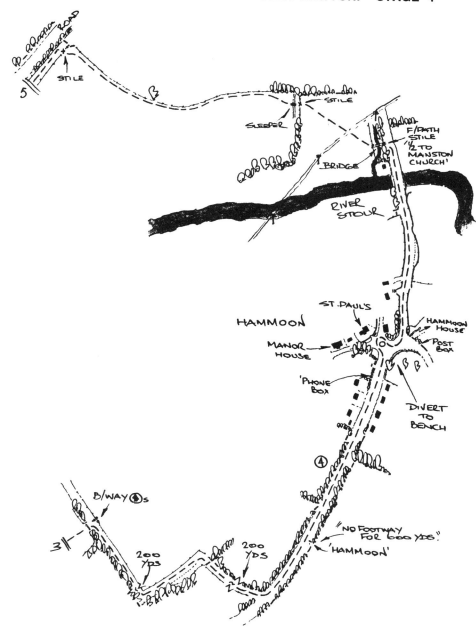

STAGE 5

MANSTON MEADOWS TO STOUR PATH

Follow the track for 200 yards to the RH gate before Manston House grounds. Go out through the gate onto the road. A confirmation footpath sign points back to 'Hammoon 1/2'. Turn left and follow the road round to the right, passing the entrance gates to Manston Church and Manston House on your left before crossing the bridge over Manston Brook.

The original 17thC Manston House was destroyed by fire in 1857 and a new one was built. At the same time, the mausoleum which you glimpsed earlier was erected. In this quiet little corner of Britain, a revolutionary event took place on 8th/9th October 1883. The first experimental cremations were conducted here as recorded, 'in a simple and inexpensive furnace and the ashes were laid in the mausoleum'. The furnace was apparently larger than suggested as it is now a listed monument as are the house and the mausoleum.

St Nicholas' church shows probably why the North aisle at Hammoon church was removed. St Nicholas' North aisle was added to the 13thC chancel in the 14thC and it stands well to the left of the aisle. It would be almost impossible to see the altar from there. When the chancel arch was narrowed in the 19thC, a squint had to be built-in for the same reason.

However, we must press on. Just over the bridge, turn left onto the track alongside the brook, signed for 'Sturminster Newton 1'. Follow the track for a few yards to a footpath-arrowed gate with the instruction 'Dogs to be Kept on Lead'. The arrow points to a wide grass track which lurches towards a gateway in the wire fence about 250 yards ahead. Manston Brook joins the River Stour over on your left. Through this next gate, follow the cattle path - a long, winding, narrow path - for 1/2 mile. Take your time as this is a lovely, pastoral stroll and aim for the far RH corner of the field - too far away to try and locate the stile or the gate which both lead out of your field from this distance.

Five minutes later, you will find the footpath-arrowed stile and concrete bridge with the gate about 50 yards to its right. If the stile is blocked or the field full of corn or anything else (it has been known), go through the gate. Whichever you use, begin to veer towards the RH hedge as, before you reach the end of this narrowing field, you will find a double stile and a narrow footbridge through the hedge and over a ditch.

On the other side, stop and look to your left. Above the slope of the hill with thistles sprouting out of it, you will see the tops of two trees and some bushes.

Turn to Stage 6 and your route will become clear.

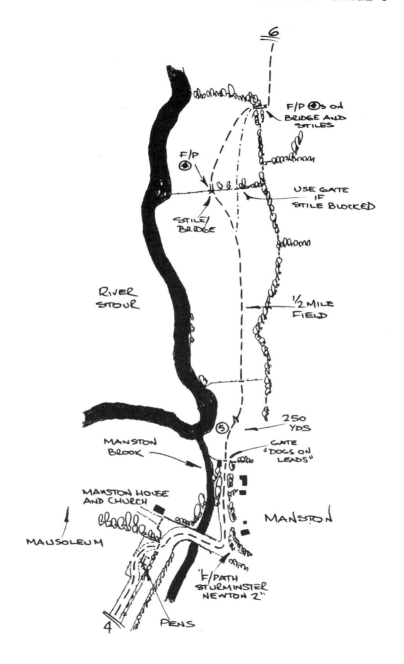

6

F/P ④s on
BRIDGE AND
STILES

F/P
④

USE GATE
IF
STILE BLOCKED

STILE/
BRIDGE

RIVER
STOUR

½ MILE
FIELD

250
YDS

⑤

GATE
"DOGS ON
LEADS"

MANSTON
BROOK

MANSTON HOUSE
AND CHURCH

MANSTON

MAUSOLEUM

"F/PATH
STURMINSTER
NEWTON 2"

4

PENS

STAGE 6

STOUR PATH TO STURMINSTER NEWTON

ROUTE 1: There are two tree tops showing over the hill to your left. Aim just to the right of the second one (see sketch) and begin your climb. In about 200 yards, you will arrive at the end of a long, broken hedge with a footpath arrow on a post. Walk down the RH side of this hedge and go past tree No 2. At the end, go over the footpath-arrowed stile in the facing hedge and over the long, concrete bridge into the next field. Keep almost straight on across this next, long field but veering slightly right to meet the hedge near its far end. Here, you will find a footpath pointer signed for 'Manston Church 1/2' the way you have come and 'Sturminster Newton 1/2' straight on. Follow the hedge around a right bend to a pair of stiles with a small bridge over Chivricks Brook between them.

In the next rising field, walk up to the gate in the top left corner. Go up the grass track and leave by the stile. Just outside on the wide grass corner verge, there is a reverse footpath sign for 'Manston 1.1/2'. Cross the road to the opposite pavement for safety's sake and, within 30 yards, cross back over to the stile which leads onto a path between two gardens, signposted 'Railway Path 1/2'.

Follow the path quickly to its end. Then emerge onto a tarmac track, signed 'Manston Road' in two directions. Cross over and go down the wide, grass track signed 'Railway Path 1/4'. At the end, go over the stile and turn half-right aiming for another stile between a hedge and some brick houses. Over this footpath-arrowed stile, aim for the steps which run up the side of the embankment ahead of you. Go through the kissing gate with the footpath arrows but don't go up the steps. Go under the railway arch instead and, on the other side, go over another stile which brings you out into a field with a hedge and fence on your right.

Follow the RH hedge to a gate and stile with a footpath arrow on your right. Here you are joined by the short cut walkers from Fiddleford Mill.

ROUTE 2: At a collection of gates and stiles, go straight past the stile which leads onto an enclosed path on your left. Go over the other footpath-arrowed stile at the end of the RH hedge instead and, in this next field, go over the stile in the LH end corner. On your left, there will be a gate with a stile next to it. Go over this one.

ROUTES 1 AND 2: Over this stile, aim diagonally across the field towards the trees with a stile lurking within them - by a footpath pointer for 'Fiddleford Manor and Mill 1' and 'Butts Pond 1/4'. Go over the stile into a shady, narrow path which soon opens out into a narrow tarmac lane with houses on either side. Walk to the Gotts Corner end and turn right into Penny's Lane. A few yards up the hill, the long stone cottage on your right is Vine House. *Here, the boy William Barnes, the greatest ever Dorset dialect poet, was given his first job as a clerk for Thomas Dashwood, the solicitor. The wrought-iron gates on the opposite corner lead into the grounds of what was once the old Endowed School where William Barnes was educated until 1814 when he left to join Mr Dashwood at the age of thirteen. The rest, as they say, is history.* Now, past the left turning to St Mary's church, keep straight on to the top of Penny's Lane and then bear right back into Market Square.

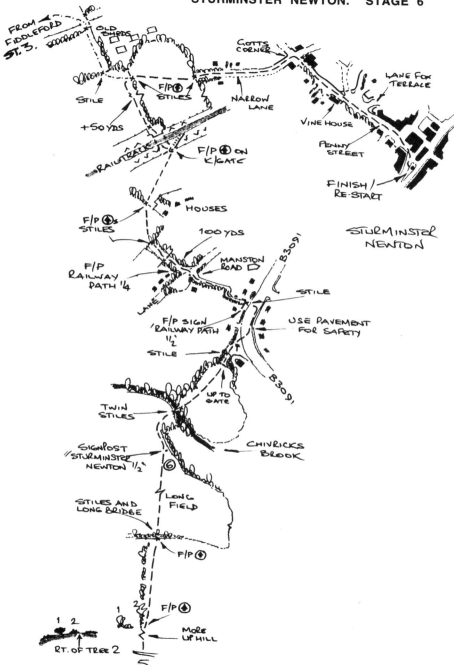

FROM FIDDLEFORD ST. 3.

OLD SHEDS

GOTTS CORNER

LANE FOX TERRACE

STILE

F/P ④ STILES

NARROW LANE

VINE HOUSE

+ 50 YDS

PENNY STREET

RAILTRACK

F/P ④ ON K/GATE

FINISH / RE·START

HOUSES

F/P ④s STILES

STURMINSTER NEWTON

100 YDS

F/P RAILWAY PATH ¼

MANSTON ROAD

B.3091

LANE

STILE

F/P SIGN 'RAILWAY PATH 1½'

USE PAVEMENT FOR SAFETY

STILE

B.3091

UP TO GATE

TWIN STILES

CHIVRICKS BROOK

SIGNPOST 'STURMINSTER NEWTON ½'

⑥

STILES AND LONG BRIDGE

LONG FIELD

F/P ④

1 2

1 2

F/P ④

RT. OF TREE 2

MORE UP HILL

2/S

PART THREE - STURMINSTER MARSHALL

INTRODUCTION

This rather different walk suggested itself whilst I was sitting on the rampart of Spetisbury Rings on the walk outlined in Part 6 in this book. Downstream from Crawford Bridge, the River Stour leads to the lovely little village of Shapwick and I remembered that the National Trust had restored White Mill near Sturminster Marshall. The views from the North West of the river are extensive and the meadow walks near Shapwick are very pleasant so, if a route could be found between Sturminster Marshall and Spetisbury Rings on the South side of the river, all would be well. As it turned out, the previously unexplored part of this circular route from Sturminster Marshall proved to be particularly pleasant, through lush dairy lands with lovely pastoral views, culminating in a delightful approach to Spetisbury Rings. So, this circular walk is presented as a fairly easy ramble with no difficult ascents and punctuated at frequent intervals with unexpected views and several moments of historical interest. The River Stour is crossed twice - by monumentally beautiful bridges three miles apart. The only river crossing between these two bridges is the Roman ford at Shapwick.

Sturminster Marshall itself appears in the Domesday Book as Sturminstre and its tenant-in-chief was Roger de Beaumont. Two mills were listed, one of them being on the site of the present White Mill. The village was surrounded by open fields until an Enclosure Act of 1845 saw them divided into smaller plots. Unusually for the area, there are several timber-framed cottages in the village, the most striking of which is the terrace of eight dwellings opposite St Mary's church on the village's North end where the walk returns.

THE ALTERNATIVES

There is just the one walk from here, starting in Sturminster Marshall, just off the A350 Blandford to Poole road. The Back Lane telephone box is the chosen start/finish point - at Reference ST949002 on O S Map No. 195. Cars should be parked carefully and thoughtfully in the village. Wilts and Dorset buses 182, 183 and Damory Coaches 310 stop at the T-junction off the A350.

ROUTE: Total distance 8.1/4 miles.

	STAGE	MILES	TOTAL MILES
1	Sturminster Marshall to Water Works	1	1
2	Water Works to Westley Wood	1	2
3	Westley Wood to Middle Dairy Farm	1	3
4	Middle Dairy Farm to Vintner's Fee	1	4
5	Vintner's Fee to White Mill	3	7
6	White Mill to Sturminster Marshall	1.25	**8.25**

ROUTE LAYOUT

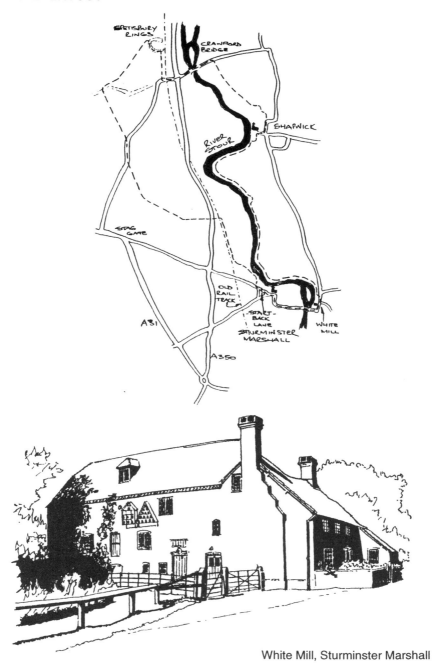

White Mill, Sturminster Marshall

STAGE 1

STURMINSTER MARSHALL TO WATER WORKS

Starting by the telephone box on the 'Back Lane' side of the green, begin by walking South West out of the village with a long thatched cottage on the wide verge on your right.   Just after the next thatched cottage, with the bus stop on the other side of the road, go past a tarmac farm track on the right and take the Bridleway-signed path immediately after it.   You will be led instantly up to the tarmac track you just passed but ours is not to reason why etc.

Follow the track between the LH hedge and the RH fenced field.   The grassy embankment seems to be a flood defence system.   Keep on until your track goes over a level bridge.   *Down on your left, there is a listed footbridge over the River Winterborne.   It is thought to date back to the 17thC and the single span is no less than 4.3/4 ft wide (1.5 m for the Euro-walkers).*

A few yards after the bridges, the track bears right and is signed 'Private Access Only'.   Here, bear left at the Bridleway arrow on the facing gate and walk up into a deep, tree-lined hollow-way.   The left side is below a high field whilst the right side is banked to protect the land and property from disrespectful gaze.   Walk up this delightfully shady track with hazels and harts tongue ferns for about 100 yards after which it begins to level out at a gate across your path.

Through the gate, and another Bridleway-signed one, there are delightful views to Badbury Rings on your right before you become entrained between hawthorn hedges for a while.   In another 60 yards, the track bears right and there is an open field on your right allowing lovely views.   On the left, the wire fence has some old concrete posts.   These are typical Railway fence posts and, as you continue, you will notice a shallow cutting followed by a levelled, grass section of abandoned track bed.   This is part of the Poole to Blandford line which you will have walked on already if you've already done Part 6 in this book.

Looking back to your left, you will see the Charborough Park tower and, a little nearer, the Black Horse Inn on the A350.

Soon, you reach the end of the field at a high block walled enclosure.   Turn left at a footpath pointer, through a wrought iron gate, and walk down to another gate with a Bridleway pointer (confusing. isn't it?).   In the next small field, bear right and aim for the opening in the wire fence.   There are painted blue arrows on the posts.   Then keep leftish of straight on, aiming past the left end of the fenced trees ahead of you.   You will find another blue arrow on the corner post.

Now, cross this short section to a farm gate which opens onto a concrete track. There are both Bridleway and footpath pointers at this gate.   I can't think why there was a single footpath pointer back there.   Anyway, turn left and walk along the level, straight track past the Water Station with its banked grassy tank.

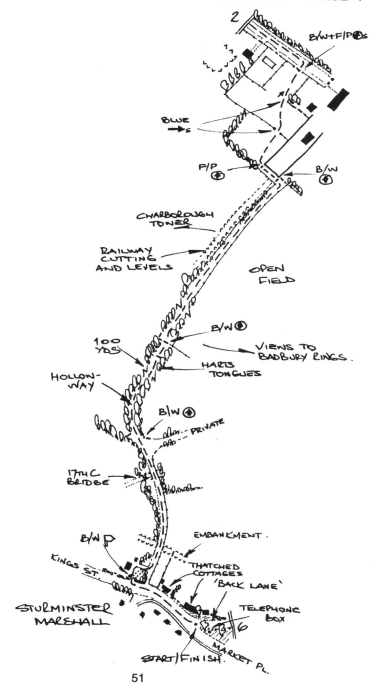

2

B/W+F/P⊕s

BLUE
→s

P/P
⊕

B/W
⊕

CHARBOROUGH
TOWER

RAILWAY
CUTTING
AND LEVELS

OPEN
FIELD

B/W ⊕

100
YDS

VIEWS TO
BADBURY RINGS.

HARTS
TONGUES

HOLLOW-
WAY

B/W ⊕

PRIVATE

17TH C
BRIDGE

EMBANKMENT.

B/W P

KINGS ST.

THATCHED
COTTAGES
'BACK LANE'

STURMINSTER
MARSHALL

TELEPHONE
BOX

START/FINISH.

MARKET PL.

51

STAGE 2

WATER WORKS TO WESTLEY WOOD

At the end of the track, stop, look and listen.   This is the A350 Blandford to Poole road and it is very busy at times.   The Water Station entrance is down on your left and there is a Wilts and Dorset bus stop opposite.   More importantly, there is a Bridleway pointer on the opposite corner where you cannot fail to notice a long, straight, grass track disappearing into the distance.   Actually, the electricity stanchion you can see at the top of the incline is 3/8 mile away.   Off you go, then.   Gird up your loins and let your mind wander as you keep straight on.

Right, you have arrived at the stanchion and found a right bend.   As the track levels out, there are glimpses of the Stag Gate entrance to the 300 acres of Charborough Park on the A31 and - not visible from anywhere else - you can see the open, low stone-wall edged lawns which were laid out below its tower. Charborough House is 1 mile distant from the Gate and cannot be seen.

Charborough House was built by Sir Walter Erle in the early 17thC but, sadly, it was burnt down during the Civil War.   It was rebuilt with materials taken from Sir Ralph Bankes' Corfe Castle which was itself destroyed by Parliament during the same war.   After the Restoration, Sir Ralph wrote to Sir Walter demanding restitution of the materials.   He seems to have been quite unsuccessful.   Sir Walter Erle built the 60 ft tower in 1790 but, after he was succeeded as incumbent of Charborough, it was struck by lightning in 1838 and much of it had to be demolished.   The estate seems to have been desperately unlucky with at least one of the three elements.   The tower was rebuilt in 1839 by John Samuel Wanley Sawbridge Erle Drax Esquire - 40 ft higher than the original.   Hence its magnificently dominating 100 ft.   The 'triumphal way' which you can see was added a few years later.   There are lovely views over on your right as well.

Now, the track undulates slightly until you arrive at a crossing of farm tracks. The left track descends and the right track goes up to the top of the hill about 20 yards away.   There are two Bridleway arrows on your RH corner before you cross over and there is another view of the Stag Gate ahead of you, down on the left.

Begin a slight descent an your grassy track, passing a clump of trees on the right before a short length of hedge.   The next trees on your right are the beginning of Westley Wood - mostly oak and sycamore.   After the first turning into the wood, you can see Charborough Farm down on your left and, practically straight ahead, you can see the 12thC church of Saint Mary the Virgin at Almer.

After the second turning into the wood, there is a more open section of track and, just past a large holly bush, the path becomes more narrow with views ahead into the next stages of your walk.

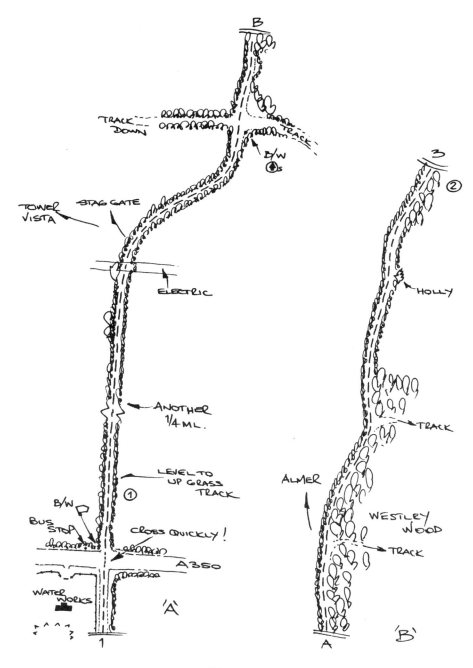

B

TRACK DOWN

TRACK

B/W
S

3

②

TOWER VISTA

STAG GATE

HOLLY

ELECTRIC

ANOTHER ¼ ML.

TRACK

LEVEL TO UP GRASS TRACK

ALMER

①

WESTLEY WOOD

B/W

BUS STOP

CROSS QUICKLY !

TRACK

A350

WATER WORKS

'A'

'B'

1

A

STAGE 3

WESTLEY WOOD TO MIDDLE DAIRY FARM

As the Bridleway opens out again, with an arrow pointing back the way you have come, you emerge onto the B3075 at a particularly shady section.   Turn right on the road and hurry along for 100 yards, crossing over to the left side just before the chevrons for those who didn't notice the bend.   There are some fine pastoral views opening up for you on the left side.   Just past the bend, there is a stile with a footpath arrow in the hedge on your left.   Go over it into the low field.

Follow the left hedge for 3/8 mile of a very gently descending field.   At the end of the hedge, go over the stile into the next field.   You may notice two vertical stones by the stile and the opening in the left hedge.   These are significant in that the stile you are just negotiating stands on the boundary between the two parishes of Sturminster Marshall and Spetisbury.   Now, continue along the LH hedge and fence for 1/4 mile to the far side of this next field.

As you near the far end, stop and look up to the hill on your front right.   You will see a barn roof with a small wood on its left.   First, there is a gap in the top hedge halfway between two electricity poles.   You will be going through that gap, so try and visualise the route from here to there.   Second, before you go, look at the trees and bushes on the hill between the next two electricity poles.   After the gap in the hedge, you will be heading for the LH end of those bushes.   (No, it's not difficult but this little insight might help you to get your bearings over the next 1/2 mile).   Now you can go.

Go over the stile in the far hedge onto the farm road and turn right.   Walk up the road past the barns of Middle Dairy Farm on your left.   After the last pair of gates into the barn yard, walk across to the left and into a small open space with a wire fence coming down to the roadside.   There is a footpath arrow in the corner which leads you into a narrow, fenced path with a sunken part of the yard on the left and a pond/slurry pit on the right.   Walk through this fenced alley and turn right at the end where a footpath arrow directs you right into a long field.   Follow the right hedge and fence up to a wire fence across your path.   Go through the 'Hampshire gate' and keep straight on up the next ascending field.

A 'Hampshire gate' is just a section of wire fence which can be easily released at one end and closed again after use.   It's less permanent than a gate but quite effective as a temporary measure.   In Hampshire, they call them 'Dorset gates'.

As you near the top, you will be able to see the gap that you need to find in the top hedge, 50 yards from the RH corner - but keep straight on alongside the hedge until you reach a narrow wood on your right.   It is steeper now and, as you reach the top, a footpath arrow directs you left along the top hedge.   Filled with confidence, follow the hedge and you'll find another 'Hampshire gate' in the gap.

Open it and go through into the next, rising field.   Remember, you want to arrive at the LH end of the long hedge on top of this hill.   So, aim 8º East of North if you have a compass.   If not, go half-left and leave the hedge at an angle of about 45º which is about half way between a level walk and the steepest climb.

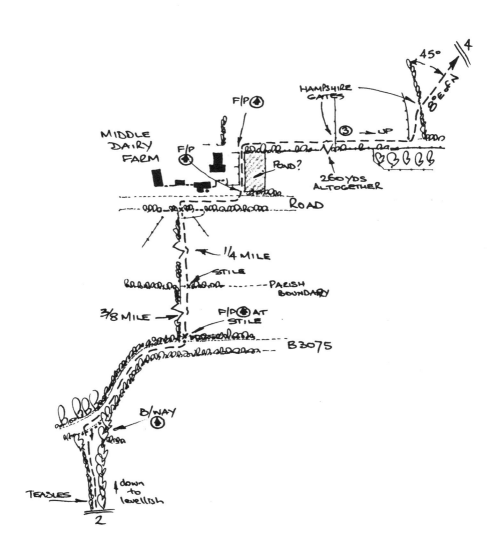

MIDDLE DAIRY FARM TO VINTNER'S FEE

As you progress up the field, more of the top hedge will appear - so will the O.S. trig point on top of Spetisbury Rings but ignore it for now.   Keep adjusting your line so that you arrive at the far left of the hedge.   You will find a footpath-arrowed stile with a top bar just wide enough to perch on and admire the fine views.

Over the stile, the footpath runs down to the gate in the far hedge.   There, a second footpath starts and runs back up this field to the gap in the ramparts of Spetisbury Rings over on your right.   If you walk circumspectly from this stile directly to the gap, I'm sure nobody will mind, but don't run and frighten the cows.

Anyway, arriving at the entrance to the rings, turn right and walk up onto the rampart.   Follow it round anti-clockwise to the O.S. trig point at a height of 255 ft with tremendous views.   *There seem to be farms all over the foreground acres as the River Stour meanders its way through the flood plains beyond the Rings. You can see Blandford from here and the tower at Blandford Army Camp.   There is another tower beyond the way you came, at Charborough Park.   Downstream, you can see Shapwick village.   That is where the next, easy mile will lead you.*

The fence at the bottom end of the Rings looks as if it cuts through the hill fort. Actually, it does.   Beyond the fence, there is a deep cutting which brought the railway through from 1857 to the mid-1960s when Dr Beeching saw fit to close the line to Blandford.   When the cutting was excavated, a 'war cemetery' was uncovered.   It was dug after the battle when the Romans overcame the iron-age defenders of this little hill fort (also known as Crawford Castle).   80 skeletons were found and, as the work continued into 1858, another 40 were discovered.

Continue around the rampart and, as you approach the bottom fence, go down from the Ring on the easiest of several paths into the ditch.   Make your way to the bottom fence and you will find a stile.   Go over the stile, cross the small clearing and walk into a sparse wood.   Keep low and wend your way through to another stile in a wire fence.   Go over into the descending field and follow the LH fence down to the bottom corner.   The railway cutting becomes an embankment on your left as you reach the bottom stile with a footpath arrow.

Over the stile, turn left into Louse Lane, Spetisbury.   Walk down to a crossroads with the A350 Blandford to Poole road with a bus stop on the far side and a bench on the verge on this side.   There are too many lorries to make the bench a suitable place for a rest so cross over the A350 and go down the opposite road.

At the bottom of the hill, you reach the magnificent, nine-arched Crawford Bridge. *The left side with the refuges from passing coaches is medieval but the right side has been widened at least twice - in 1719 and again in 1819.*   Continue along the road for about 200 yards.   Opposite a gate on the left with just enough room for a single car to park, there is a gate and stile on your right.   Go over the stile and stand still for a while as you search out the next stile which is a good 1/2 mile away in the next wire fence.   These are the meadows which lead you to Shapwick.   The path across the field is quite clear most of the time but, for the professionals, take a line just to the left of the single post (107º ESE).

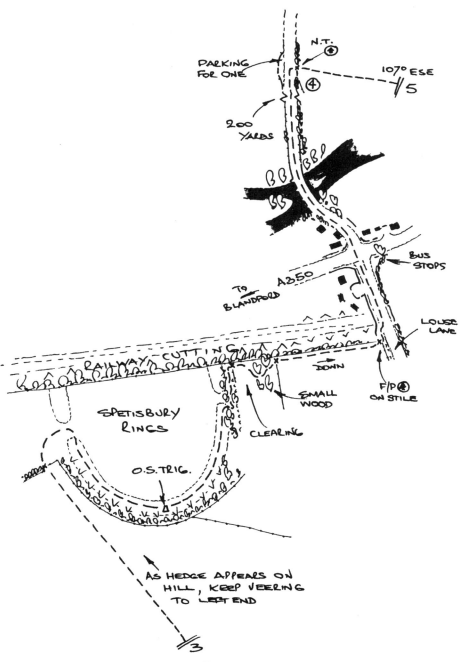

N.T.

PARKING FOR ONE

④

107° ESE

//5

200 YARDS

BUS STOPS

TO BLANDFORD A350

LOUSE LANE

RAILWAY CUTTING

DOWN

SMALL WOOD

F/P④ ON STILE

SPETISBURY RINGS

CLEARING

O.S. TRIG.

AS HEDGE APPEARS ON HILL, KEEP VEERING TO LEFT END

//3

STAGE 5

VINTNER'S FEE TO WHITE MILL

The next village is Shapwick. *By 1268, Shapwick had a market and a fair and 3000 acres of manorial lands. The Crown levied an annual rent of £140 and the services of three knights for it. The Earls of Leicester held the land at that time and they settled three knights in sub-manors of Shapwick called 'Fees'. The pasture which you are traversing at the moment was owned by Walter de Vynere and it consisted of 12 acres.* This is Vintner's Fee.

It is exactly three miles from here to White Mill and this is probably the longest Stage on one page in the book. This is just because it is so easy to find the way. The National Trust own all of this land and they have kindly installed excellent stiles with arrows all the way. So, cross the first field, aiming just left of the electricity post. At the N.T. stile in the next fence, bear slightly left to an angle of 74º ENE (about 30 yards right of the next single post and passing under the overhead wires en route). At the third stile, keep to the same line (about 25 yards to the left of a single oak) and you will arrive at the corner of the wire fence where it leads down to a track out of the field via a gate with N.T. arrows. As you are crossing the field, this gate is hidden by the little wood on your left.

Through the gate, follow the track for 250 yards towards a brick cottage. Zigzag left/right through the yard and leave by the stile to the left of a pair of gates. Keep to the drive/track which is now tarmac and keep straight on to the road with the superb 1857 Bishop's Court on your right. *There are some late 16thC parts at the back. This was the first sub-manor, named Shapwick Champagne after the Earl of Leicester's knight, Henry de Champagne. The house is called Bishop's Court after Archbishop Wake of Canterbury who bought it in 1750.*

Keep to the road through Shapwick village, past the old school on your right and Old School Cottage on your left. Soon, you reach the Anchor Inn for a respite. Turn right at the Inn, passing between the market cross and the telephone box. Follow the lane round towards St Bartholomew's Church. *There has been a church here, close to the Roman ford across the River Stour, since the 11thC. The North wall is 12thC, the tower is 14thC and the rest was rebuilt in 1880.*

Before the church gates, there is a flood defence gate in a stone wall on the left. This leads into the car park where you will find a N.T. stile in the far RH corner.

One word of advice, warning, information - call it what you will. This path has been hard won from private landowners and will continue to be available at their discretion. You are mostly required to follow edges of fields for the next 2 miles unless you are directed across a corner by the N.T. arrow. Sometimes, as in this first field, the next stile is clearly visible but you are requested not to aim straight for it but to go round the edge as shown by the arrows. After the twin stiled bridge out of this field, bear right and enjoy your long riverside stroll. There are another eleven crossings before you reach Stage 6 (three of them doubles with bridges between) and the way is perfectly signed - even allowing for diversions around the cows. So, go quietly and you will probably see coots, kingfishers, herons, moorhens, ducks and dragonflies. I'll see you on Stage 6 just before you reach White Mill.

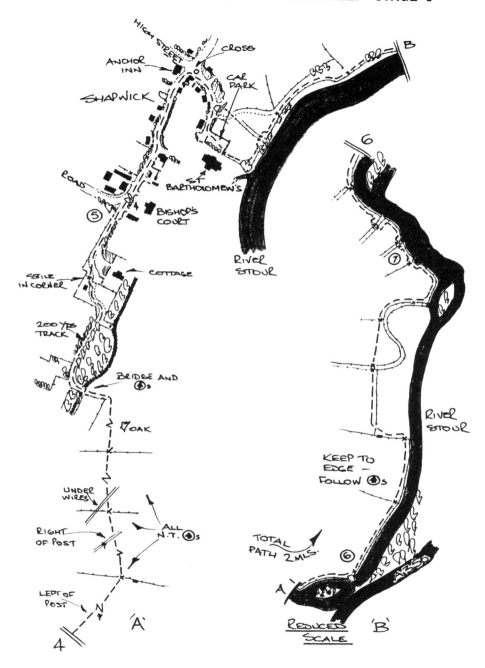

STAGE 6

WHITE MILL TO STURMINSTER MARSHALL

The field narrows to just 15 yards wide towards the end and, over the stile next to the gate, follow the hedge on the LH bank to some steps which lead up to the last stile before you join the road. Be careful. It's 2 miles since you encountered any traffic. Over the stile, turn right onto the road and walk down to see White Mill. *The building dates back to the late 18thC. A stone over the mill race is dated 1776.* Just around the next corner is White Mill Bridge.

For a sight of this beautiful bridge, go over the N.T. stile in the fence after the Mill and follow the path for a few yards. As you look back, the structure and decorative stonework appear far more beautiful than can be appreciated from above. *There has been a bridge over the River Stour here since at least 1174 and this structure is said to be the oldest in Dorset.*

Now, cross over the bridge, taking shelter in any of the 7.1/2 refuges either side on the way if necessary. Each refuge on the upstream side is built on top of a cutwater. These cutwaters are repeated on the downstream side but mainly in the interests of symmetry. They do help to reduce the turbulence but not all bridges have tapered stonework on both sides. Anyway, stroll along the level road for 1/2 mile, keeping to the right most of the way and walking on the verge when you reach the kerbed section on a right bend.

Around the bend and past a crossing of sunken tracks, there is a row of thatched cottages on your left followed by Church Farm on your right. As the road bends back to the left, the long row of cottages over on your left is listed. *'Church Cottages' is a terrace of eight dwellings. The 17thC timber frame of No 6 is still showing on the outside but the others are 18thC extensions. The next obvious landmark is the Parish Church of St Mary. Inside, the North Arcade still retains its 12thC pillars. There were additions made in the 15thC but the whole building was drastically restored in 1859 under Henry Woodyer, architect.*

Past the church, bear right into Back Lane - so called because it takes you back to the start. Walnut Tree Field leads down to the river on your right and, if you were very observant as you followed the Stour on the N.T. path, you may have noticed it from the other side at least an hour ago. However, you can now see the telephone box on the green and you have finished a lovely 8.1/4 mile walk through a most beautiful pastoral landscape.

White Mill Bridge from N.T. riverside path

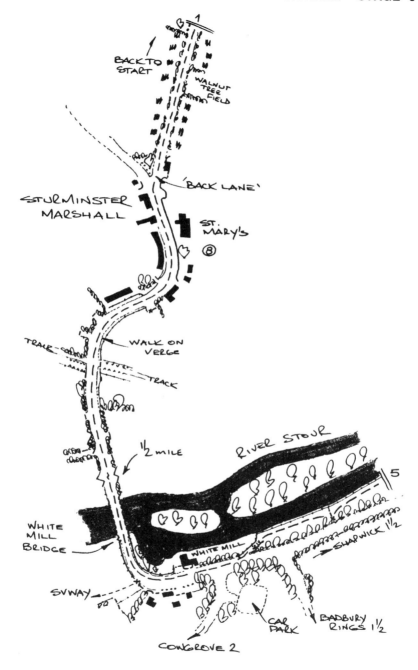

1

BACK TO
START

WALNUT
TREE
FIELD

'BACK LANE'

STURMINSTER
MARSHALL

ST.
MARY'S

⑧

WALK ON
VERGE

TRACK

TRACK

½ MILE

RIVER STOUR

5

WHITE
MILL
BRIDGE

WHITE MILL

SHAPWICK 1½

SV WAY

BADBURY
RINGS 1½

CAR
PARK

COWGROVE 2

PART FOUR - THROOP AND PARLEY

INTRODUCTION

Considering the proximity of this part of Dorset to the sprawling urbanity of Bournemouth, this is a surprisingly lovely walk across some fine dairy farmland, along a superb stretch of the River Stour and past some beautiful listed farm buildings. There is a fine flour mill which was powered by a water-turbine. There are moorhens, swans, grebes and wild ducks. There is a turbulent weir and fishermen quietly pitting their wits against the plentiful fish and the caprices of the river. There are grassy paths across fields and well-signed farm tracks which bring you close enough to Bournemouth International Airport to provoke a longing to be off on a sun-drenched holiday. There are cows, horses, bison, Vietnamese pot-bellied pigs and golfers practising their swings. That's right, bison. For some years, Parley Court Farm has been home to a small group of bison and you may see them as you pass through. The pot-bellied pigs are at the children's farm at Merritown. So, with rooks overhead and the clear river coursing its last few miles to the sea, this is a walk of many surprises

Throop is located 1 mile North of the A3060 Castle Lane which runs from the A338 Bournemouth Spur Road to the Bournemouth suburb of Redhill. The easiest way is by turning right (from the A338 direction) at the Broadway Inn into Broadway Lane and following it to Throop Road at its end. Throop Mill car park is at Reference SU112958 on O S Map No. 195.

ROUTE: Total distance 5.3/4 miles - Starting at Throop Mill and negotiating its sluice gates, the walk crosses a short field to a huge weir before finding quieter fields and tracks to Merritown Farm and the Alice in Wonderland park (summers only). A field on the ancient river terrace leads to a path around the edge of the Golf Range before Parley Court Farm. There, you will find horses and cows (and the bison, if you're lucky) before crossing level fields with Bournemouth Airport close by and the occasional aircraft dropping in above you. A short stroll on a country lane leads you past Bramble Farm and over more fields to New Road, Parley. An easy amble down New Road leads you over the River Stour at Ensbury Bridge to a pleasant 1.1/2 miles long stretch of riverside walking nearly all the way back to Throop Mill.

STAGE	MILES	TOTAL MILES
ROUTE 1:		
1 Throop Mill to Malmesbury Fields	.75	.75
2 Malmesbury Fields to Parley Court Pond	.75	1.5
3 Parley Court Pond to Church Lane	.75	2.25
4 Church Lane to Throop Mill	3.75	**6**

ROUTE LAYOUT

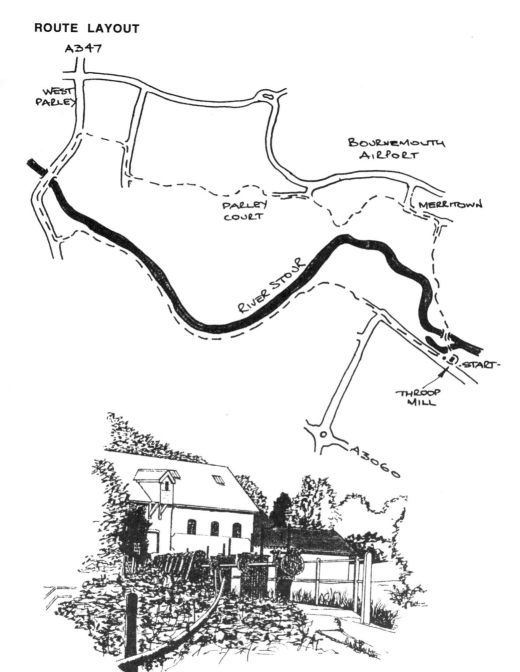

Throop Mill from the Footpath

STAGE 1

THROOP TO MALMESBURY FIELDS

Originally powered by water and, towards its end, by turbine engines, corn has been ground at a mill on the Throop Mill site for nine hundred years. When the mill race was laid out to its present form in 1944, ancient stone foundations were discovered and coins from the reigns of Georges III and IV were found, together with other Spanish and Portuguese coins. For a short history of the Mill, have a look at the notice board in the Car Park.

Leaving the Car Park, walk down Throop Lane and go past the Mill to a Footpath signpost near the steps which proclaims 'Public Footpath. West Hurn. 1.1/2'. Go down the steps and follow the footpath to the back of the mill. The path turns left and follows the edge of the entrained river to the concrete path over sluice gates between the head waters and the river pool. *It is only in the recent past that the route of the Stour, which used to follow this top level and was the cause of frequent annual flooding, was diverted to the route which you will soon cross by a modern footbridge.*

Passing the 'Fishing Permit Holders Only' path on your right, keep to the signed, gravel 'Public Footpath' as it turns across the open grassy area with river on either side and you'll arrive at a steel bridge across the Stour with all sorts of level controls and a weir which causes wild turbulence underneath. On the other side, turn left at the Footpath sign for 'Merritown 1' and cross the small bridge over a stream and a stile with a Footpath pointer on the other side.

After a pleasant stroll alongside the river, enjoying the grebes, the moorhens and the reedbeds, the path bears slightly right and heads for the stile in the end of the field fence where it meets the river's edge. Over the stile, follow the river more closely now, with a few bushes and willows right in the water when it is running deep. If you are wondering what the roaring noise is, Bournemouth International (Hurn) Airport is just beyond the fields to the North of the approaching Merritown Farm. Anyway, over the next stile by the river's edge, turn half-right and cut across the field to the next stile in the far corner.

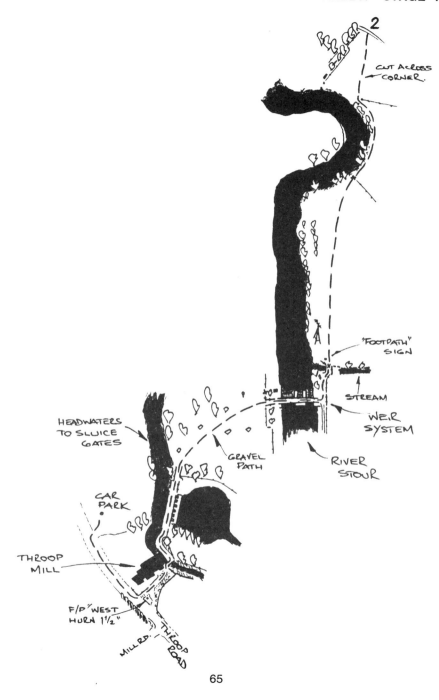

2

CUT ACROSS
CORNER.

"FOOTPATH"
SIGN

HEADWATERS
TO SLUICE
GATES

STREAM

WEIR
SYSTEM

GRAVEL
PATH

RIVER
STOUR

CAR
PARK

THROOP
MILL

F/P "WEST
HURN 1½"

MILL RD.

THROOP ROAD

65

STAGE 2

MALMESBURY FIELDS TO PARLEY COURT POND

At the stile in the corner of the field, climb over into a very wide grassy track between high, parallel hedges.   The track is reduced to more conventional width by deep bushes and brambles.   Keep on along the track for about 200 yards with high old oaks on either side and with comfrey and nettles growing in season.   At an ancient oak wood on your left, which now sports pine trees and encroaching rhododendrons as well, the track loses its grassy covering and becomes less pleasant in the last part where the mud is frequently kept from drying out completely by the shade of the overhanging trees.

Emerging now, over a stile by a farm gate onto a junction of a left farm track and a right tarmac lane - and with a steep bank facing you - turn left at the 'Public Footpath' arrow and go past the sign on the uphill, gravel track 'Private. Merritown Farm. Public Footpath Only'.   Through the personnel gate next to the farm gate across the track, keep straight on with a descending field on your left and a complex of fun-farm enclosures on your right.   Continue straight on through the Merritown Farm buildings, taking special note of the farmhouse on your right.

The high brick house is the central section of a formerly grand house which had vast wings at either end but which were pulled down in the late 18thC.   It was part of the estates bought by Lord Malmesbury in 1800 and the farmhouse still retains some superb Georgian panelling.   Unfortunately, this is the rear of the building but the front elevation has a particularly fine Georgian frontage with a huge stone staircase and pillars either side of the main door.   The ice-house has long since fallen into disuse and has become completely overgrown.

Keep straight on through the farmyard and, as the track turns right, go over a stile by the farm gate facing you and follow an undulating route close to the banked hedge on the RH side of the field beyond the stile.   A deep drainage ditch runs parallel with the path down on your left.   When you reach another stile, by an electricity post with a yellow painted arrow, at the end of the hedge, climb over and turn instantly left to walk between the high protective bank of the Golf Course and Driving Range on your right and a hedged and fenced bank down into the field you have just left.

Follow the guard bank and the fence and keep on round to the right as you briefly come close to the edge of the Stour again.   Past the office and buildings of the Range and Golf Course, join a tarmac drive past the 4th tee.   After a fenced paddock on the RH side and past a signpost for 'Church Lane 2', the tarmac drive turns away to the right at a junction with a gravel farm track on the left.   With a postbox on the RH corner, turn right and instantly sharp left again, going through a farm gate or the adjacent half-gate across the tarmac drive which runs past a gated cattle grid.

Follow the lane alongside the RH fence and beech hedge with Parley Court Pond on your left.

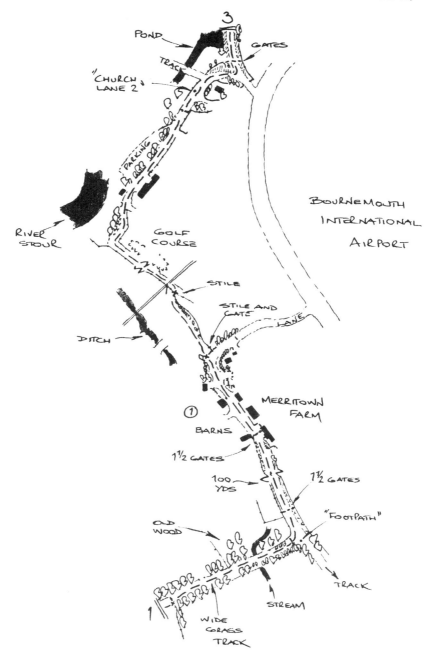

3

POND

GATES

TRACK

"CHURCH LANE 2"

PARKING

RIVER STOUR

GOLF COURSE

BOURNEMOUTH INTERNATIONAL AIRPORT

STILE

STILE AND GATE

LANE

DITCH

MERRITOWN FARM

① BARNS

1½ GATES

100 YDS

1½ GATES

"FOOTPATH"

OLD WOOD

TRACK

STREAM

1

WIDE GRASS TRACK

STAGE 3

PARLEY COURT POND TO CHURCH LANE

Past the pond and a farm track which comes in from the left, go through the gate by another cattle grid and keep on the wide drive past a couple of houses on your right. This wide track, now with a ditch on either side, promises an easy walk but you have to leave it temporarily because the farm which straddles it is not open to visitors. However, a perfectly adequate detour for walkers is provided, starting at the 'Private' and 'Public Footpath' signs by the next yard on your right.

Go into the yard with a small stable around to your right and you will see a gate at the RH end of the fence facing you with a 'walking man' sign to confirm the walkers' route. Go through the gate into the horse trials practice area and turn left up the grassy incline around the back of a cottage. At the top of the slope, with a Leylandii hedge bordering the garden on your left, go over the stile in the fence and cross the farm track, past another 'walking man' post, into the next field which has a long brick shed as its LH boundary.

Just after a cattle trough, a stile in the fence on your left takes you back onto the wide gravel drive. Turn right onto the track for a few yards, away from the beautiful Georgian Parley Court Farm house, and follow the track until the wire fence ends at a gate. Immediately after the boundary hedge of the field you have just left (Field 1), there is an adjacent gate and a stile with a Footpath arrow. Go over the stile and follow the clear grass edge of the field in front of you (Field 2). Don't go through the gap into the field on your immediate left (Field 3).

Keep closely to the hedged edge of Field 2 as it bends round left and then go over the stile by a farm gate with another yellow arrow ahead of you in the LH corner. Along the edging fence of the next long field, you arrive at a farm gate in the far LH corner. Over the gate, keep close to the RH hedge, past three gates and a cattle trough inserted into it near its far end. Go over a stile by another farm gate in the RH corner by another 'Public Footpath' pointer into a long farm track between high hedges.

At the end of the track, go over the stile by the gate where, by the gate on the left into Snooks Farm, a signpost advises that it is 1.1/2 miles on the Footpath from Christchurch Road. Turn right onto Church Lane, opposite Church Farm Cottages, and follow the hedged lane, past 'Stour Park' house, Brambles Farm and another fine, brick house on the left.

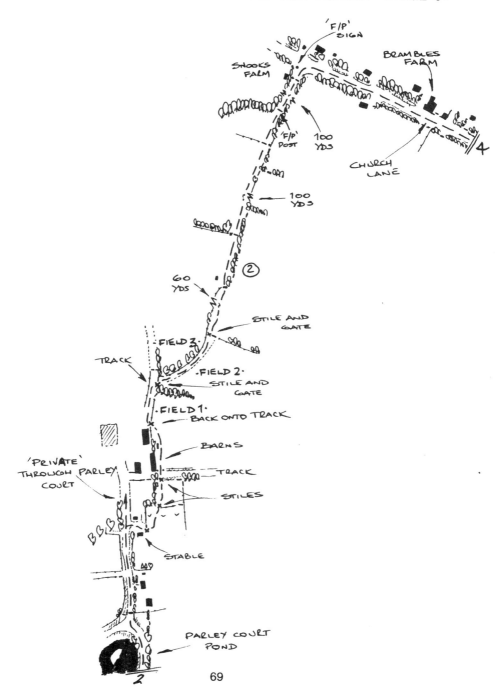

'F/P'
SIGN

SNOOKS
FARM

BRAMBLES
FARM

'F/P'
POST

100
YDS

100
YDS

CHURCH
LANE

②

60
YDS

STILE AND
GATE

·FIELD 3·

TRACK

·FIELD 2·

STILE AND
GATE

·FIELD 1·
BACK ONTO TRACK

BARNS

'PRIVATE'
THROUGH PARLEY
COURT

TRACK

STILES

STABLE

PARLEY COURT
POND

STAGE 4

CHURCH LANE TO THROOP MILL

In a few yards, turn up the gravel track signed 'New Road 1/4' and go over the stile onto a path which runs at first alongside another hedge on your left.   As the LH hedge and fence run out, keep straight on across the field with a wire fence on your immediate right.   A sign at the start of this fence implores you to 'Keep to Public Footpath'.   At the far end of this field, you reach a stile in the fence. Climb over by the 'Footpath. Church Lane 1/4' pointer into New Road, Parley.

Turn left and follow the pavement past houses and left and right fields.   Just after the River Stour comes into sight you cross Ensbury Bridge.   *The bridge was built to replace one which collapsed soon after the First World War.*   Keep on down New Road, now completely suburban, cross Greenacres Close and take the next left into Brecon Close.   At the end of the close, bear left onto the Footpath which runs between the fence of Water Lane Farm and the wood on your left. *Variously used for housing homeless people, as a riding school and a donkey sanctuary, the converted and extended farm is now privately owned.*   On reaching the river, turn right through a strange chicane and begin a 1.1/2 mile easy amble through the 'Stour Valley Local Nature Reserve'.

The River Stour was causing Bournemouth Corporation a lot of concern in the 1960s as its South bank was eroding and threatening houses and gardens in Redhill.   By 1975, the Wessex Water Authority had taken over responsibility and a new channel had been cut, the old river bed had been filled in and the area had been levelled.   To overcome the frequent flooding in this area, controlled tipping of environmentally friendly waste was arranged and, by 1982, when the work was finished, the bank was raised to its present level.

Keep straight on alongside the river until the path leaves its banks and heads inland on a well-defined and enclosed path.   When you see the Wessex Water Holdenhurst Sewage Purification Works, go through the kissing gate and through the gate on its right.   You are only on the gravel track for a few steps before turning left through another kissing gate onto another clear Footpath.   About 50 yards later, you emerge through one final kissing gate onto a tarmac drive.   Keep straight on along the drive for about 1/4 mile and you will soon arrive at a lovely little cottage on your left.   *This is Muccleshell Farm which has its own claim to fame.   Dating back to 1587, and once known as Muccleshell Hall, it is thought that Charles II spent a single night here in 1651.*

Immediately after the farmhouse, you will be ejected into Throop Lane with Broadway Lane joining you from your right.   Walk along Throop Lane, past Hicks Farm on your left and a mixture of old cottages and newer housing on your right. Keep straight on, past the turning into the new estate on your right and past Throop Mill Cottage on your left until you arrive back in Throop Mill Car Park.

The adjacent map omits all of the riverside walk from the Water Lane Farm chicane to the 'Water' Works kissing gate, partly because it's perfectly easy to follow but mainly to save another two pages.   This walk is an extra bonus to those originally planned for this book and it was only squeezed in at the last minute.   I'm sure you will have followed it all right though.

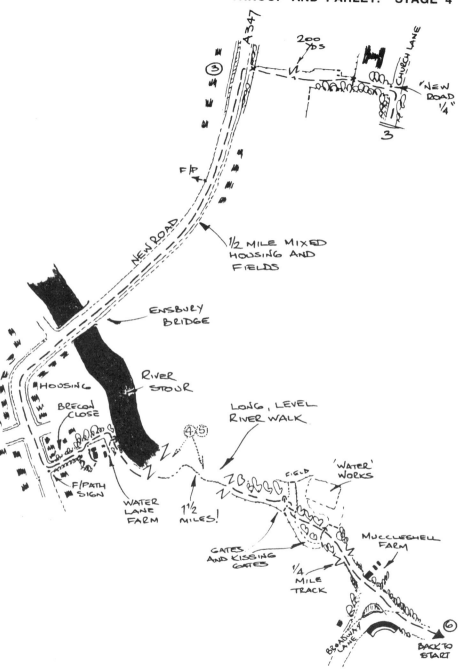

PART FIVE - PIDDLETRENTHIDE

INTRODUCTION

The village of Piddletrenthide manages to include both names of the little river in its title. Known variously as the River Piddle and the River Trent, it rises about 2 miles away in Alton Pancras before wending its independent way to the sea. It doesn't run into any other rivers on its way but manages to stay aloof all the way into Poole Harbour near Wareham. It isn't the one that flows by Wareham Quay. That's the River Frome. The Piddle shuns the town and stays outside the walls to the North of the town. The name comes from the Saxon *pidelen* or *pedel*, meaning low land on marsh or water.

Appearing in the Domesday Book as *Pidrie*, during which time the land was held by St Peter's, Winchester, there were three mills within the parish. Sadly, the name appears to have upset the Victorians who set about changing the names of the villages along the route of the river between here and Wareham. Hence, Puddletown, Tolpuddle, Affpuddle, Briantspuddle et al. Luckily, they seem to have missed Piddlehinton and Piddletrenthide.

Starting in the village near The Piddle Inn at Ref SY705997 on O.S. Map 194, this 5.1/4 mile walk visits two vastly different villages and their character churches. In between, the path leads you over some of the most stunningly beautiful chalk downland with deep valleys, ancient fields and long views towards the distant coast. On the way round, the walking changes from level strolls to steeper climbs up ridgeways, from country paths to ancient high downs tracks and village lanes. With a fine Manor House to see as well, there is something here for everybody and, with the skylarks twittering above and the buzzards mewing even higher, the high fresh air is particularly stimulating.

Although a lovely walk at any time of the year, it is particularly fine from late Autumn to Spring because the sun is lower and the Romano-British settlement on West Hill and the scattered field systems can be seen to better advantage.

Parking is only possible in the main B3143 but this is quite a long and straight road through the village and there is ample kerbside space South of the Piddle Inn. Just park with care and consideration and you will be perfectly all right. If you would prefer to use public transport to get to Piddletrenthide, there are frequent No. 307 buses running from Monday to Saturday from Dorchester and Sturminster Newton.

	STAGE	MILES	TOTAL MILES
1	Piddletrenthide to Kiddles Bottom	.75	.75
2	Kiddles Bottom to West Hill	1.25	2
3	West Hill to Plush Hill	1.25	3.25
4	Plush Hill to Piddletrenthide	2	**5.25**

ROUTE LAYOUT

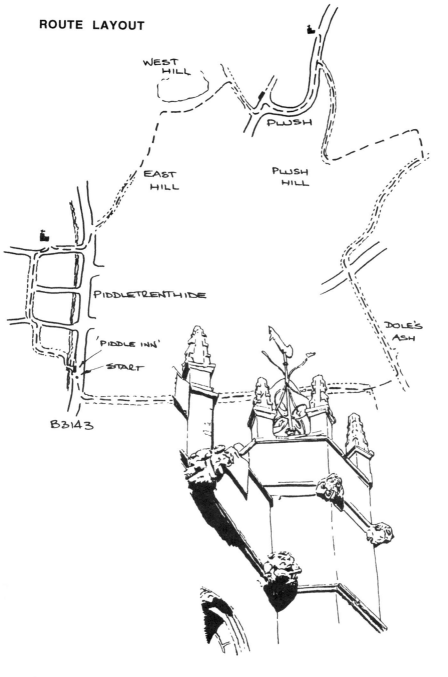

WEST
HILL

PLUSH

EAST
HILL

PLUSH
HILL

PIDDLETRENTHIDE

DOLE'S
ASH

'PIDDLE INN'

START

B3143

All Saints' Parish Church, Piddletrenthide - Page 76

73

STAGE 1

PIDDLETRENTHIDE TO KIDDLES BOTTOM

Originally, the village was built around All Saints' Parish Church but this is now about 1/2 mile away from the starting point of this walk. A great fire on 2nd May 1654 destroyed much of the old village and rebuilding seems to have favoured a line closely following the course of the River Piddle. Nearly every cottage had a source of fire-extinguishing water right outside the door.

Having made your way to the Piddle Inn, walk up the Bridleway-signed path to follow the River Piddle round the back, passing the pub garden and car park on your way to a little bridge with a Bridleway arrow on the far end. Cross the river and walk carefully along a wide, grassy track between hedges. This part of the Bridleway is sometimes a little churned up by the horses but you will soon be on firmer ground. After two open barns on your left and a huge old barn with an extended threshing floor in the walled yard, the track turns right and becomes gravelled.

The track still runs between hedges but there are now high fields on your left and gardens dropping down towards the river on your right. Follow the track, past a few houses on the right, including the twin-gabled Trent House with its brick and flint-walled garden. At the end of the track, a Bridleway sign points back along the track. Turn left into the rising, banked road. Within a few yards, turn right onto a flint track between hedges. A Bridleway pointer confirms the way. Follow the widening track which, after the fine square Manor House in the lawned garden down on your right, acquires a parallel path on your right.

The rendered, slate-roofed Manor House was built in the late 18thC by one of the last members of the Collier family, the principal family in Piddletrenthide for many years. The lease of the Manor House passed to the Bridge family in 1812 and they added a third storey in 1832. Before that, there had been a balustraded parapet above the second storey. The Bridges were famous jewellers and one of their number made the Crown of State for Queen Victoria. In the park, there is a 27ft high 18thC dovecote and an octagonal 19thC gazebo. The gazebo has six bas-relief casts showing scenes from Homer.

This path accompanies the track past a brick and flint cottage but fades out before the track descends after a barn on the left. When the lane turns off to your right to the B3143, keep straight on, rising again, and becoming hedged in on both sides. The sunken path has come back on the right but it is deeper and seems more like a narrow hollow-way. Keep straight on. The fields up on your left are at the lower end of Kiddles Bottom, one of the coombes which emanate from the ridge overlooking Cerne Abbas to the West and the Piddle Valley on the East.

Soon, the track descends and widens as you keep straight on - neither looking to right nor left - between some rather nice houses and gardens.

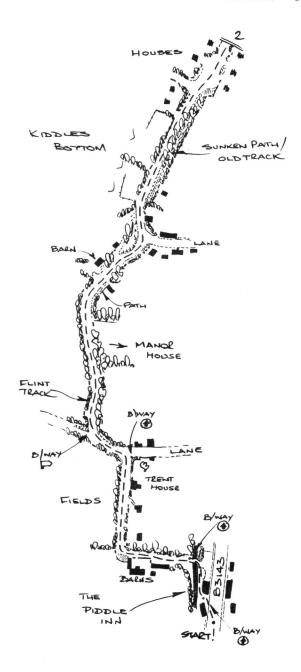

HOUSES

2

KIDDLES
BOTTOM

SUNKEN PATH/
OLDTRACK

LANE

BARN

PATH

MANOR
HOUSE

FLINT
TRACK

B/WAY

LANE

B/WAY

TRENT
HOUSE

FIELDS

B/WAY

B3143

BARNS

THE
PIDDLE
INN

START!

B/WAY

75

STAGE 2

KIDDLES BOTTOM TO WEST HILL

At the end of the track, turn right and go down the bending lane.   Just around the corner, go up the sloping path and have a look at the Parish Church of All Saints.

Even if you don't go inside All Saints', the hordes of mythical animals which adorn the buttresses, the tower, the string courses and the dripstones should not be missed.   The internal doorway in the 15thC porch is the oldest part of the church. It is 12thC.   The ornate tower was built in 1487 whilst the North and South walls of the church are of about 1500.   The rest of the exterior walls are early 15thC, just predating the tower.   There is a small sundial above the porch door but it appears to be about 20 minutes slow.

The church was restored in 1852-53 by John Hicks.   If that name seems familiar, this was the architect who taught young Thomas Hardy the trade which took him to St Juliot's in Cornwall where he met his first wife, Emma Gifford.

Back in Church Lane, keep on down, between some very pretty cottages and, after the bridge over the Piddle, walk up to the B3143 again.   Turn left and walk carefully along the road for 100 yards.   Take the Footpath-signed track on the right, just before the 30mph derestriction signs.   After passing through two farm gates, take your time up this grassy as it wends its way up the side of East Hill. First, you pass a small chalk quarry and then you are entrained between banks where the track has been worn down over the hundreds of years it has been in use.   There are good views back to Piddletrenthide and along the valley towards Buckland Newton as you keep walking up the side of the ridge.

At the top of the track, go over the Footpath-arrowed stile in the hedge facing you.   The paths are usually very clear across the cultivated fields around here but, if this one is uncertain, walk very slightly right away from the stile.   For the technical, the stile faces North-South and the path runs up and over the hill at about 24º to 22º ENE as you cross.   There are skylarks everywhere.

At the top, keep straight on, aiming between a distant trough and a green water tank.   *Look over to your right to see the shadowed ridges of an ancient settlement on the next ridge, Plush Hill.   The RCHM interprets these levelled areas as sites for groups of huts.*   Arriving at the far side of the field, bear left to follow the hedge.   In just 30 yards, turn right and go over the Footpath-arrowed stile.   Bear right, towards the hedge and join the green track.   You are now skirting around the South-East side of West Hill.

The ridges on your left are the remains of strip lynchets, a later field system which cuts into the distinctive ridges of the Romano-British settlement.   There are many more strip lynchets along the field over the hedge on your right but these are better seen from Plush Hill when you get there later.

Keep on down the track and go through the Footpath-arrowed gateway at the end of the hedged section.   Stay on the higher of the two green tracks.

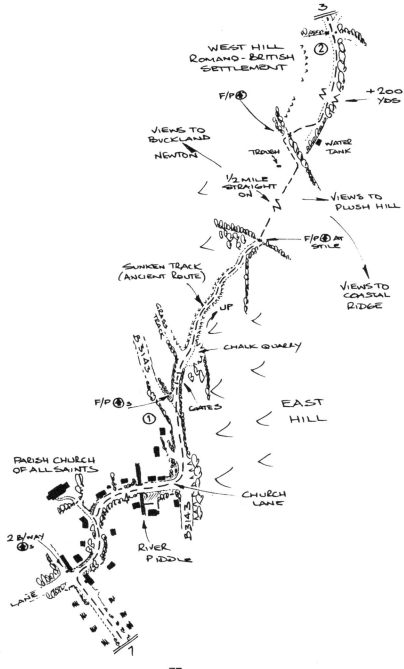

3

WEST HILL
ROMANO-BRITISH
SETTLEMENT

②

F/P④

+200
YDS

VIEWS TO
BUCKLAND
NEWTON

WATER
TANK

TROUGH

½ MILE
STRAIGHT
ON

VIEWS TO
PLUSH HILL

F/P④ AT
STILE

SUNKEN TRACK
(ANCIENT ROUTE)

VIEWS TO
COASTAL
RIDGE

UP

GRASS TRACK

CHALK QUARRY

B3143

F/P④s

GATES

EAST
HILL

①

PARISH CHURCH
OF ALL SAINTS

CHURCH
LANE

B3143

2 B/WAY
④s

RIVER
PIDDLE

LANE

1

STAGE 3

WEST HILL TO PLUSH HILL

The track soon bears a little to the right and descends to meet a chalk track with Bridleway and Footpath arrows.   The Bridleway runs up to Alton Pancras on your left.   However, turn right and follow the sunken track down to the bottom where a gate and stile lead onto a tarmac lane.   Turn left where the sign advises you that this is 'Plush'.   Walk down the lane to the T-junction with the 'Plush 714022 finial.

Originally a tithing which belonged to Buckland Newton, Plush was joined to Piddletrenthide in 1933.   The Brace of Pheasants on your left was formerly two semi-detached 18thC cottages.

Turn right, signed for 'Mappowder and Hazelbury Bryan' and wander down the lane past the Old School House.   At the bottom, the lane bends left and begins to climb up again.   Walk slowly uphill until the lane passes 'Millers Barn' on your left and the sign tells you that you are leaving 'Plush'..

The lane is now sunken between high, tree-clad banks with vast amounts of harts tongue ferns on either side.   Keep walking up the steeper hill, past a Footpath-arrowed gate on your right and the stone gateway to Plush Manor House on your left.   You are going up here to visit the Church of St John the Baptist, a little further up on the left, before coming back to this gate and going up to the ridge.

St John the Baptist is a 'different' sort of church.   It was designed by Benjamin Ferry in the 'Decorated' style and was built in 1848.   The earlier church which it replaced stood a little further away up this same road.   The present church owns some of the plate from the earlier one but, apart from that, it is completely Victorian.   Externally, it is quite plain and it doesn't have a tower.   However, it has a particularly fine twin bell-cote.   There is a good view of the valley and surrounding hills from the West end of the church.   Actually, unless my compass was being affected by some unseen power, the church lies South-East to North-West rather than East to West.

Back at the Footpath-arrowed gate down the hill from the church, go through and begin to ascend the Plush Hill on the steep chalk and grass track.   On the way, look back for an excellent view of *Plush Manor House, a lovely Georgian building with rendered walls and a fine slate roof.*   Near the top, the track bends round to the left to meet a Footpath-arrowed stile in the wire fence.   This leads into a high, large field and you can't see the exit stile just yet.   So bear half-left, aiming 30 yards left of a small tree on the horizon (124º SE).   After 200 yards, you arrive at a Footpath-arrowed stile in the LH hedge.   Climb over and bear a little left of the direction from which from you arrived (104º E) - aiming for the right hand end of the row of trees over the horizon.

Just past a concrete water tank, you arrive at a gate with a Footpath arrow in a wire fence.   Through the gate, keep straight on (100º E) across this shorter field, aiming for the space between two clumps of trees ahead.   You arrive at a corner on the edge of the wood.   Turn right and follow the edge of the mixed beech and sycamore wood downwards, soon joined by a wire fence.   At the end of the fence, turn right onto the track which comes from your left.

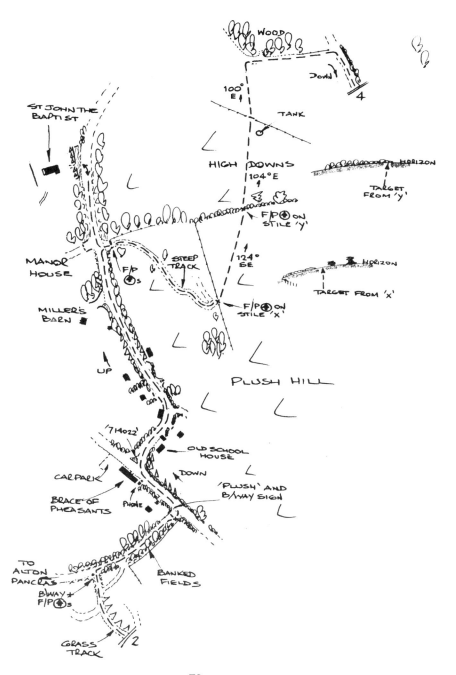

WOOD

DOWN

100° E

TANK

ST JOHN THE BAPTIST

HIGH DOWNS
104°E

HORIZON

TARGET FROM 'y'

FP ON STILE 'y'

MANOR HOUSE

F/P S

STEEP TRACK

124° SE

FP ON STILE 'x'

HORIZON

TARGET FROM 'x'

MILLER'S BARN

UP

PLUSH HILL

'714022'

OLD SCHOOL HOUSE

CAR PARK

DOWN

'PLUSH' AND B/WAY SIGN

BRACE OF PHEASANTS

PHONE

TO ALTON PANCRAS

BANKED FIELDS

B/WAY + F/P S

GRASS TRACK

2

STAGE 4

WEST HILL TO PIDDLETRENTHIDE

In about 300 yards, the LH hedge turns away to the left and the track is joined by a wire fence on the right (at a Bridleway arrow). Keep walking down for another 500 yards. The track then passes through a hedge with a Bridleway arrow on a nearby post. Keep on down the open field for another 500 yards. The track bends to the right at an area of rough ground with a hedge behind it. Keep straight on with this hedge for yet another 500 yards.

At the end of the track, carefully cross the road and cross the driveway which leads to 'Doles Ash Cottages'. Go past the Bridleway pointer and join the path that runs alongside the RH hedge with the electricity posts spaced on your side. Another 500 yards of slightly descending walking brings you to an area of brambles and rough scrub with Doles Ash down on your left.

Doles Ash Farm itself is the twin-gabled house nearer our path. The house was built in the 17thC but was extensively modified in the 19thC. That is why the front which faces our route is so pleasantly Georgian. The converted barns and stables date back to the 17thC and 18thC.

Keep straight on and join the track which comes up from Doles Ash. There are now sweet chestnuts along the track on your right.

In just 100 yards, take the narrower, hedged-in track on your right. If you find yourself near a small wood, you've gone too far. The narrow track is probably unsigned but it is the right way. It may be a bit lumpy because of the horses but you'll soon be on firmer, wider tracks. No sooner said than done. Over the brow of the hill, you join a wider grass track which comes in from your left. Now begins a most pleasant, mile long downhill stroll back to Piddletrenthide. The track is hedge-in most of the way but it is so wide and on a downward slope that there are extensive views nearly all the way.

The track becomes flintier and passes a large, three-bayed barn before ascending slightly. From the top of this short rise, it is all down again, becoming concrete for the last, steeper section.

After you have passed a Footpath going off to your right, you soon reach the B3143 again. The sign confirms that you have just come down 'Tullons Lane' whilst the Bridleway arrow confirms your direction. Turn right and make your way back to your vehicle, bus or car. This has been an exceptional walk, especially with the high downs, the skylarks and the buzzards.

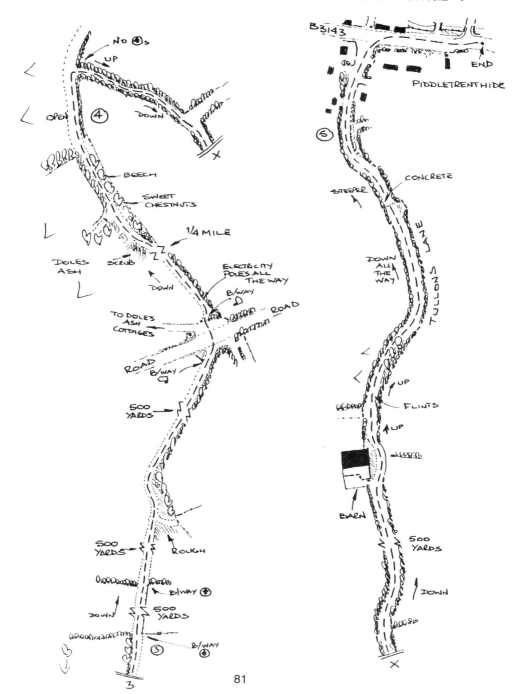

No ④s
UP
<
OPEN
<
④
DOWN
X
L
BEECH
SWEET CHESTNUTS
1/4 MILE
DOLES ASH
L
SCRUB
DOWN
ELECTRICITY POLES ALL THE WAY
B/WAY
TO DOLES ASH COTTAGES
ROAD
ROAD
B/WAY
500 YARDS
500 YARDS
ROUGH
B/WAY ④
DOWN
500 YARDS
⟳
③
B/WAY ④
3

B3143
END
PIDDLETRENTHIDE
⑤
STEEPER
CONCRETE
DOWN ALL THE WAY
TULLONS LANE
<
UP
<
FLINTS
UP
BARN
500 YARDS
DOWN
UP
X

81

PART SIX - SPETISBURY

INTRODUCTION

Although this particular favourite is hard pushed to make 3.1/2 miles, there is so much variety packed into it that it would be seriously negligent to leave it out of a book of favourite walks. There is something here for everybody - the amateur archaeologist, the historian, the artist, the naturalist, the train spotter and anybody who just enjoys wonderful views and an exciting, yet mostly easy walk.

The walk begins and ends near Spetisbury First School and immediately takes you for an easy stroll along the railway line which Dr Beeching closed down in the 1960s. Actually, I lied about the train spotting but, if you use your imagination, you can visualise one of the great steam monsters trundling through the cuttings and pulling into Spetisbury Station where the platforms are now almost overgrown with brambles and shrubs.

The contrast with the next part of the route couldn't be more marked. A sudden step back in time brings you to Iron Age Spetisbury Rings (a.k.a. Crawford Castle) which was overtaken by the invading Roman army under Vespasian.

After crossing the River Stour over the medieval Crawford Bridge, easy field paths lead to the site of the dissolved Tarrant Abbey and the beautiful little 12thC Church of St Mary with its fine 13thC wall paintings. Easy, level walking on bridleways and footpaths alongside the Rivers Tarrant and Stour then leads to Keynston Mill before the route crosses a wide flood plain with many little bridges over tributaries of the meandering Stour. A stroll through Clapcotts Farm brings you to the A350 Blandford to Poole Road which you cross to return to the start.

THE ALTERNATIVES

There aren't any proposed here. This is, as they say, probably the best walk in the area. The walk starts and finishes in the West End lane near the side entrance to Spetisbury First School - Reference ST098030 on O S Map No. 195. Park well over to the LH side of the road towards the Railway bridge. If you're using the bus, Wilts and Dorset's 182, 183 and Damory Coaches 310 from Bournemouth, Poole and Blandford are fairly frequent.

ROUTE : Total distance 3.1/2 miles.

STAGE	MILES	TOTAL MILES
1 West End to Spetisbury Rings	1	1
2 Spetisbury Rings to Tarrant Abbey Gate	1	2
3 Tarrant Abbey Gate to Keynston Mill	1	3
4 Keynston Mill to West End	0.50	3.50

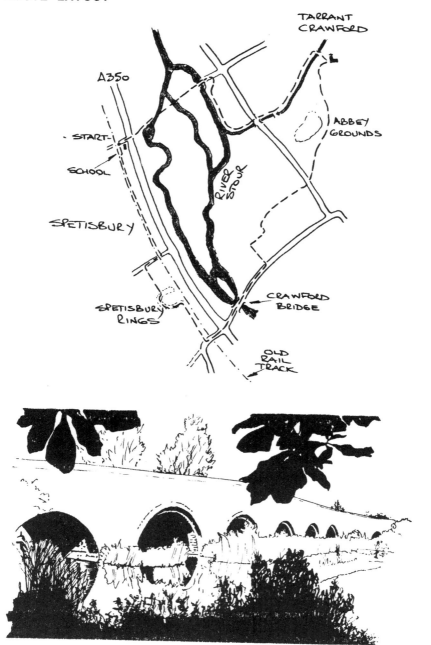

Medieval Crawford Bridge

STAGE 1

WEST END TO SPETISBURY RINGS

Walking away from the hustle of the A350, take the half-gate in the LH hedge onto the gravel path which rises to the top of the old railway embankment.   It is signed for the Stour Valley Way.   On the track, turn left and you will soon be walking along a grassy path in the deep cutting.   There is about 3/4 mile of this easy walking, so just settle down and enjoy the bird song from the encroaching bushes and trees.

With glimpses of an old cob-walled garden down on your right and good views over the Stour Valley on your left, you soon arrive at the deserted Spetisbury Station.   There is a little roofless brick shelter with a wooden seat half-way along the RH platform but, if you sit there forever, there won't be any trains arriving. Anyway, come back to the beginning of the platform and turn right to find some grey brick steps down to the road under the bridge.

Turn left on the road and walk up the hedged lane.   About 100 yards up the lane, go round a farm gate in the LH hedge through a gap with two footpath arrows.   In the rising field, follow the direction of the LH arrow, aiming for the entrance into the hill fort ahead of you.   As you reach the gap, turn up the RH ridge of the Iron Age Spetisbury Rings and walk around its rim towards the O.S. Trig Point at 255ft above sea level.

This is a fine place to stop and admire the extensive views all round but, before you begin to look into the distance, there is more at your feet.   Down the slope, the fence at the other side of the hill fort runs along the top of the 1857 Railway cutting.   *During the cutting, 80 skeletons were found in a mass grave and further work in 1858 produced another 40.   Experts consider that the deaths were the result of an attempt to defend the fort against the advancing Roman hordes and that the grave may be a war cemetery similar to that at Maiden Castle near Dorchester.*

Now, the views.   There are several farms scattered about whilst, at 22ºNNE, you can see Tarrant Keynston village.   Then, clockwise, Shapwick is at 85º with the Isle of Wight far beyond it.   Bournemouth is behind the big tree on your right and, still rotating, the tower at Charborough Park is clearly visible at 158ºSSE. Turning round towards the way you arrived, Blandford is low down at 326ºNW with Melbury Downs above it in the distance.

The open fields and the Stour Valley which is beyond the Railway cutting look inviting so, regretfully tearing yourself away from this lovely spot, keep walking around the rim of the Rings.   Nearing the bottom fence, find your way down the easiest route you can find off the rampart and go over the stile in the bottom corner against the Railway cutting fence.

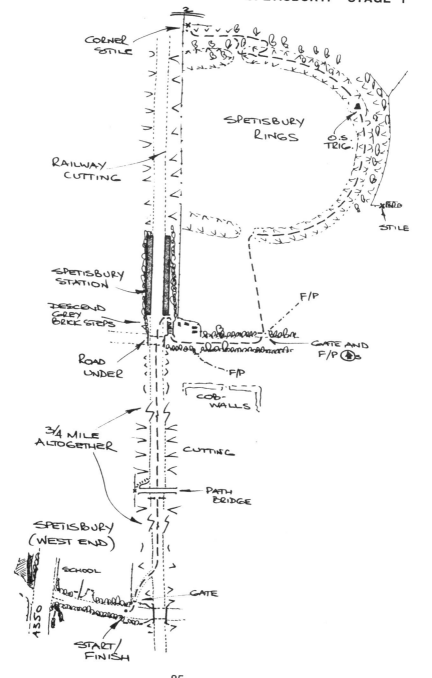

CORNER STILE

SPETISBURY RINGS

O.S. TRIG.

RAILWAY CUTTING

STILE

SPETISBURY STATION

F/P

DESCEND GREY BRICK STEPS

GATE AND F/P s

ROAD UNDER

F/P

COB-WALLS

3/4 MILE ALTOGETHER

CUTTING

PATH BRIDGE

SPETISBURY (WEST END)

SCHOOL

GATE

A350

START/ FINISH

SPETISBURY RINGS TO TARRANT ABBEY GATE

Walk across the clearing and into a tangled, narrow wood.   Wend your way through to find another stile which lets you out into a descending field with the cutting down on your left.

At the bottom of this field, go over the stile in the LH corner and drop down the short path into the road.   This is the strangely named Louse Lane.   Turn left and pass between the buttresses of the old Railway bridge as you walk down to the busy A350.   If you need a rest, there is a bench on the wide grass verge on your right - but this is really meant for bus travellers.   You could always sit on the grass.   However, it's a bit noisy here so cross over instead and descend, between some cottages on your left and a raised garden on your right, towards the long and beautiful, nine-arched Crawford Bridge.

The West (upstream) side of Crawford Bridge dates back to medieval times but the other side was rebuilt in 1719 and again in 1819 when the road was widened.

Here, the River Stour runs from two channels through the flood plains upstream of the bridge into a single wide flow on the downstream side of the bridge.   Both views are rather fine and you could spend a few peaceful moments looking into the River in the haven of the four refuges from passing carriages.

Leaving the shelter of the bridge, walk along the road for about 100 yards to a gate with just enough room to park one car for a future visit.   In another 50 yards, you reach a half-gate in the LH hedge and fence.   Go though the Bridleway-arrowed gate and walk straight across the field, aiming for the left end of the facing hedge.

When you arrive at the corner, turn sharp right (Bridleway-arrowed) and follow the hedge past a large tree and an electricity pole until you reach the wire fence at the other end.   Turn left and go over the stile by the gate with a Bridleway arrow and, in a complex of gates, turn right up the wire-fenced track to pass between the legs of an electricity stanchion.

At the top of the track, go over a pair of stiles on either side of the private Water Company road and continue up the opposite field, keeping close to the LH hedge.

At the top of this last field, go over another stile next to a pointer which shows that a Bridleway follows the hedge parallel to the road.

Cross over the road and go over another stile, next to a Bridleway-arrowed gate, into a high field with a grass track following the line of a row of telegraph poles.

You have now entered part of the empty grounds of Tarrant Abbey which was dissolved by Henry VIII during the Dissolution of the Monasteries.   The Abbey was founded in the late 12thC for a small community of nuns - but more of that on the next Stage.

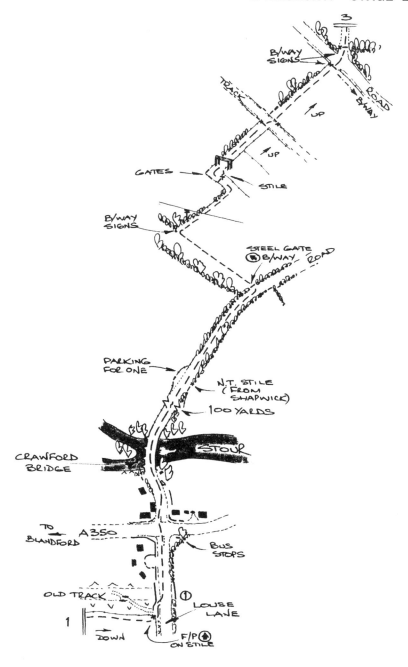

STAGE 3

TARRANT ABBEY GATE TO KEYNSTON MILL

Follow the grassy track, with the field dropping down on your left, to go over a stile next to a Bridleway-arrowed gate across your path.   Go over the stile and follow the descending track past a disused quarry on your right and with the Abbey grounds down on your left.   You won't see anything of the Abbey as it was completely destroyed and all that now remains are a few scarps and banks in amongst the farm buildings and Tarrant Abbey House down below you.

At the bottom of the track, go over another stile and keep straight on, diagonally to the main farm track over on your left, aiming for a gate much nearer the Church of St Mary which you can now see.   As you go, look back along the farm track towards the farm buildings.   The long, low buttressed brick building which you can see is known as the Norman Barn although its oldest parts are mainly 14thC and the buttresses themselves are 18thC brick.

Reaching the half-gate, go through and turn right along the track to visit the Parish Church of St Mary.   *There was a convent church as well as St Mary's and this was where Bishop Poore was buried in 1237AD.   This was the Bishop whose vision saw the beleaguered occupants of Old Sarum remove to the new, lower site by the River Avon in Salisbury.   There he began the building of the magnificent Salisbury Cathedral but he so loved this little community at Tarrant Crawford that he wanted to be buried here and not at Salisbury.   In 1238, Henry III's sister, Queen Joan of Scotland was also buried here but, as the convent church did not survive, nothing can be found today.*

12thC St Mary's was carefully restored in 1911 and, for more complete details, I would suggest you buy a leaflet before you leave.   Suffice it to say, the wall paintings are of the 13th and 14thC and they were only discovered during the 1911 restoration.   The main fourteen scenes depict the incredible sufferings of St Margaret of Antioch and her eventual arrival in Paradise.   There are other scattered paintings all over the place but the leaflet will explain them all more clearly.

Now, leaving St Mary's, cross over the track and go over the River Tarrant by the substantial steel and concrete bridge.   Follow the tarmac track all the way to rejoin the drive from Tarrant Abbey House and follow it straight on to the road which you crossed on the previous Stage.

Cross over it again and go through the footpath-arrowed gate into the vineyards of Keynston Mill.   Follow the LH edge of the plantation clockwise, following the Tarrant and then the Stour, and zig-zagging under some electricity stanchion guy-wires on the way.   Having passed the vines first and the soft fruits last, the path bends around a small group of trees before depositing you on a lane with the Farm Shop and Car Park opposite.

Turn left down and follow the lane down to a ford in the river on your left and a fine house with an enveloping wisteria on your right.   Cross the narrow bridge, made from rescued rail tracks and concrete.   Mind your head on a low, overhanging branch as you go.   Walk straight ahead across the water meadows

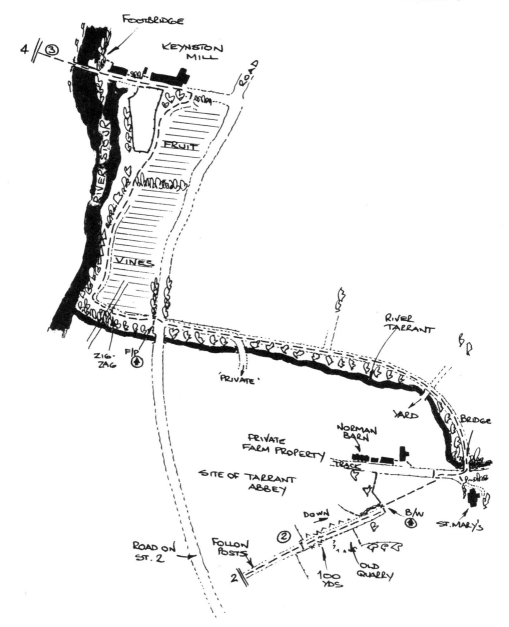

STAGE 4

KEYNSTON MILL TO WEST END

The River Stour divides into three more or less equal parts as it runs through this flat flood plain.   Keynston Mill is built on the first part and Clapcotts Mill is built on the last part almost 1/3 mile away on the other side.   The third channel flows centrally between the two whilst the little boggy ditch which you are now approaching will probably dry up completely in the next few years.

After the boggy ditch, walk on for another 100 yards to cross the middle channel by another rail track and concrete bridge with young trees on either bank. Keeping straight on, there are views to Spetisbury Rings ahead of you, over to your left.

Eventually arriving at the far side of the flat plain, go through the gate with a footpath arrow onto a narrow, meandering path with nettles and scrub on either side.   Crossing the sluice gate which serves the now defunct Clapcott Mill, you arrive in a gravel yard of the converted mill.   This is a now private residence so walk on quickly and quietly, following the arrows on the brick wall of the little bridge so that you zig-zag right/left through the yard.   The driveway runs slightly to the left after the bridge but walk up onto the long, low footbridge with the footpath sign just to the right of the drive.

The gardens are lovely but try and enjoy them circumspectly as you keep walking over the bridge, respecting the owners' privacy.

Soon, you arrive at the exit end of the driveway by a wooden garage.   Keep straight on and join the gravel drive as it runs between the LH fenced field and the barns and cottages of Clapcotts Farm on your right.   The rubble-stone middle part of the farmhouse dates back to the 17thC.

At the end of the farm track/drive, you come out onto the A350 Blandford to Poole road and, crossing over, you arrive back in the lane where you started this lovely walk.   I hope you enjoyed it and learned a lot on your way round.

St Mary's, Tarrant Crawford - Page 88

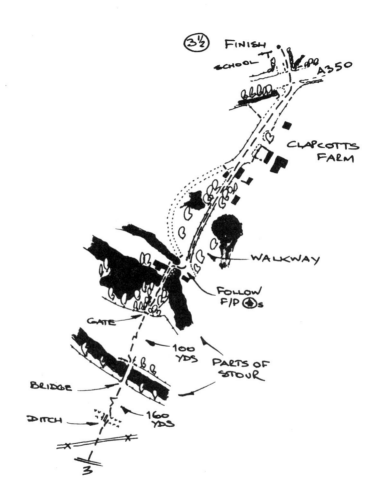

PART SEVEN - THE WIMBORNE STOUR

INTRODUCTION

The market town of Wimborne Minster keeps cropping up as a superb centre for walking through some of the most pleasant countryside in Dorset.   It features in *'Circular Dorset Rambles'*, it is the start and finish point for *'The Cranborne Chase Path'* and it is passed closely by *'The Stour Valley Way'*.

THE ALTERNATIVES

In this selection, there are two Options for mainly level walks of either 4.3/4 or 7.1/2 miles.   Both of the walks begin at the Tourist Information Centre in the High Street (Ref. SZ009000 on O.S. Map 195) and, somewhere along the line, meet up with 'The Stour Valley Way.   Leaving Wimborne, and after a stroll through meadows and along a pleasant country lane, Route 1 continues by crossing the river near a Roman ford to visit the hamlet of Cowgrove and the elevated (and listed) village green of Pamphill where village cricket is still regularly played. Route 2 leaves Wimborne to visit Cowgrove and Pamphill by a more direct route.

ROUTE 1: Total distance 7.1/2 miles - This walk takes you through the centre of Wimborne and along the Poole road to Canford Bridge where 'The Stour Valley Way' joins you.   You then go West along field footpaths and a demoted main road through farming country to Lake Gates.   From Lake Gates, the path crosses wide meadows to Eye Bridge near where the Romans crossed the River Stour on their way from Badbury Rings to Hamworthy (Moriconium).   Crossing the Stour on Eye Bridge next to the Roman ford, a choice of easy strolls along a country lane or along the River Stour brings you to Cowgrove Common and, past a typical village duckpond, you follow an ancient hollow-way called All Fools Lane to the village of Pamphill.   From Pamphill, you descend through woods and grassy fields to find and follow the edge of the River Stour back into Wimborne.

ROUTE 2: Total distance 4.3/4 miles - Beginning at the T.I.C., this route leads directly to the River Stour and follows the upstream path to Eye Bridge before visiting Cowgrove and Pamphill.   After returning to Eye Bridge with Route 2, the easy path leads straight back into Wimborne.

To get to Wimborne, the buses from the major towns include: - Poole - Wilts and Dorset 132, 133, 183 and X32.   Bournemouth - Wilts and Dorset 132, 133, 182 and 183.   Blandford and Shaftesbury - Wilts and Dorset 182 and 183.

Once you've left Wimborne's vast assortment of refreshment facilities, you won't pass any more shops, tea-shops or pubs until you reach Pamphill.   Then you can leave the path for a few hundred yards to partake of a cream tea or stock up with country provisions at the very popular Pamphill Dairy Farm Shop.   Just tell them I sent you and I'm sure you'll be well looked after.

STAGE	MILES	TOTAL MILES
ROUTE 1:		
1.1 Wimborne to Canford Bridge	1	1
1.2 Canford Bridge to Merley Hall Farm	1	2
1.3 Merley Hall Farm to Lake Gates	1	3
1.4 Lake Gates to Cowgrove	1.75	4.75
1.5 Cowgrove to Pamphill School	1.25	6
1.6 Pamphill School to Stour Path	1	7
1.7 Stour Path to Wimborne	.50	**7.50**
ROUTE 2:		
2.1 Wimborne to Eye Bridge	1	1
1.4 Eye Bridge to Cowgrove	1	2
1.5 Cowgrove to Pamphill School	1.25	3.25
1.6 Pamphill School to Stour Path	1	4.25
1.7 Stour Path to Wimborne	.50	**4.75**

ROUTE LAYOUT

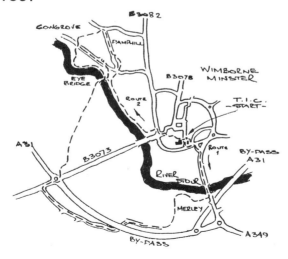

ROUTE 1 - STAGE 1

WIMBORNE MINSTER TO CANFORD BRIDGE

About 713 AD, a Benedictine nunnery was founded by St Cuthburga where Dean's Court now stands and Wimborne's Norman Minster Church with its mid-15thC West tower is built on the site of the original abbey church. Wimborne was already an important settlement known as Wymburn or Winburnham because of its position on the River Wym where it joined the River Stour. In 871 AD, after the battle with the invading Danes at Martin, near Cranborne, King Alfred the Great buried his fatally wounded brother Ethelred here.

High up on the North wall beyond the porch, you will see the Quarter Jack who was carved in 1613 dressed as a monk. Since the Napoleonic wars, he has sported the livery of a Grenadier. He is connected to an entirely separate mechanism from the amazing astronomical clock inside the church.

Time to go now so turn down High Street and follow the low churchyard wall, leaving the traffic to zig-zag along the road. This passage takes you between the Minster and the 1906 stone-built Church House to emerge into King Street, opposite the Methodist Church and No 5 which is a medieval timber-framed house and one of Wimborne's oldest domestic buildings. Turn left and follow the road past Deans Court Lane. *Here, on the site of the medieval Deanery and the Manorial Court, the superb Deans Court was enlarged in 1725 and rebuilt in 1868.*

You are now in East Street and one branch of the divided River Allen runs under the road from your left to emerge somewhere beyond the houses on your right in Deans Court Park. *The River Allen rises away to the North near Monkton-up-Wimborne on Cranborne Chase and, passing through Wimborne in two parts, it joins up again to run into the River Stour at Canford Bridge.* Past Millstream Close and The Rising Sun, the second stage of the Allen flows under your feet at Eastbrook Bridge. *The sign 'Safety First. Do Not Stand on the Bridge' recalls the dangerous days when this bridge carried all of the traffic, carts and carriages through Wimborne from East to West and back. It's quieter now since they built the By-pass.* Anyway, passing the left turning towards the Cricket Ground, keep straight on into the pedestrianised part of East Street, past the old Post Office to Poole Road corner and turn right.

Follow this short section of Poole Road until it joins the main Poole Road traffic. Now keep to the pavement alongside the iron-railed flood defence walls which keep the River Stour from invading this low part of Wimborne during times of particularly high river levels. Just past an estate cottage by double iron gates, continue past the thatched Coach and Horses. *Not too long ago, a mummified cat was found in the roof beams.* There are tempting views of the Stour plains through the railings as you progress along Poole Road and you'll be heading off that way in a few minutes *New Borough Road, over on the left, leads to Wimborne's very popular Market which is held on Fridays, Saturdays and Sundays every week.*

Carry on past Station Road and cross over Canford Bridge where there are lovely views along the Stour in both directions. On some warm summer days, you may see rowers and skullers from nearby Canford School training on the River.

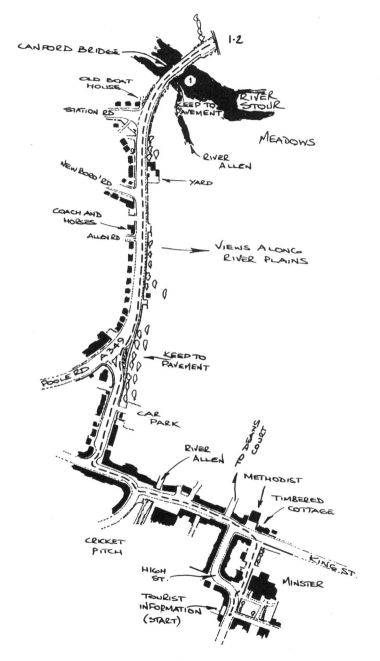

CANFORD BRIDGE

1·2

OLD BOAT HOUSE

RIVER STOUR

STATION RD

KEEP TO PAVEMENT

MEADOWS

RIVER ALLEN

NEW BORO' RD

YARD

COACH AND HORSES

ALLEN RD

VIEWS ALONG RIVER PLAINS

POOLE RD A 349

KEEP TO PAVEMENT

CAR PARK

RIVER ALLEN

DEANS COURT

METHODIST

TIMBERED COTTAGE

CRICKET PITCH

KING ST.

HIGH ST.

MINSTER

TOURIST INFORMATION (START)

CANFORD BRIDGE TO MERLEY HALL FARM

This three-arched Canford Bridge was built in 1813 although one has existed here for centuries and it has been extended to cover the flood-plains on either side as well as the River Stour itself. After the steel-railed footway, sheltered from the thundering traffic by the old stone bridge walls and the newer stone-capped brick walls, Footpath Numbers 92 and 30 over on your left lead onto Lady Wimborne's Drive to Canford Magna. After the second house on your right, turn into the passageway which is signed 'Footpath 31 Lake Gates'.

Through the passage, at another 'Footpath 31' sign, you emerge into a housing estate at Merley Ways. *Perhaps I should explain here about The Stour Valley Path and The Stour Valley Way. In 1994, I completed researching and preparing my first long-distance guided walk book entitled The Stour Valley Path and, within days of publication, I found that Dorset County Council were working on a similar project which they were going to call The Stour Valley Way. After the initial panic, it transpired that my route was similar in some places but quite different in others and that, whilst mine was completed by using already existing public rights of way, theirs would take several more years to finish because new footpaths were to be created and new routes negotiated with landowners. By 1999, the official path hadn't penetrated as far as Blandford Forum whilst The Stour Valley Path went all the way to Stourhead. Late in 2000, both routes were combined in a unique collaboration between Green Fields Books, Greenlink and the Stour Valley Project.*

Now, keep straight on, passing Derwentwater Road on your left and, when the road bends left, turn right into a passage, signed 'Footpath 31 Lake Gates'. This leads down to a lovely little playground where mums and kids can rest or play away from the traffic on the edge of beautiful countryside. Keep straight on through the park and go over the heavy railway-sleeper stile at the top. Follow the RH fence with the River Stour below you on the other side of a small wood.

Arriving at a Stour Valley arrow, go over the stile and follow the LH wire fence along the top of a river terrace until the fence turns left. Follow it to climb over another signed stile into a narrow path between the fenced field and a wood of hazel and oak on your right. At the top, you meet Willetts Lane where you turn right and follow it between a banked LH hedge and the wood on your right. The white line acknowledges its earlier role as a route from Lake Gates to Canford before the By-pass gave it everlasting peace. Follow the lane and descend along the LH bank of the By-pass to a junction of wood fences and gates at the bottom of the slope. Through the gates, ignore the gated grass track straight ahead and go under the By-pass to the ascending lane up the other side.

You emerge into a turning area with several Bridleway and Stour Valley arrows and a signpost for 'Footpath 31 and Bridleway 114' pointing back the way you came. Keep straight on along the hedged lane, passing a cattle-gridded gateway, a greenhouse and some sheds on your right. *Merley Hall Farm is of particular interest as, between the twin main sections of the brick-built house which abut the lane, there resides, in much splendour, a Dutch-style gable end complete with its own resident saint.*

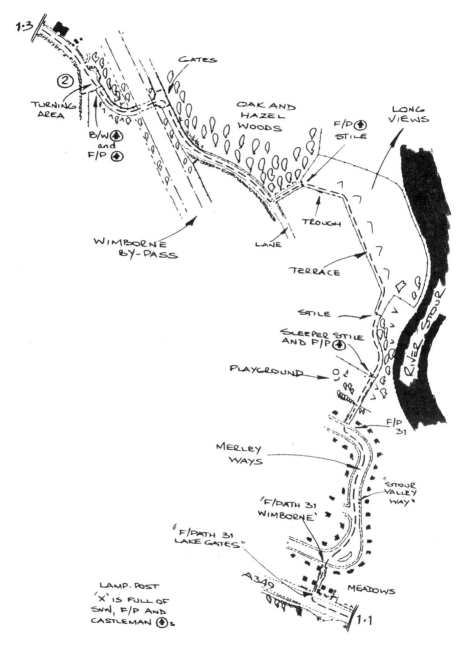

1·3

②

TURNING
AREA

B/W ⊕
and
F/P ⊕

GATES

OAK AND
HAZEL
WOODS

F/P ⊕
STILE

LONG
VIEWS

WIMBORNE
BY-PASS

LANE

TROUGH

TERRACE

STILE

SLEEPER STILE
AND F/P ⊕

PLAYGROUND

R. VER STOUR

F/P
31

MERLEY
WAYS

"STOUR
VALLEY
WAY"

'F/PATH 31
WIMBORNE'

'F/PATH 31
LAKE GATES"

LAMP. POST
'X' IS FULL OF
SWW, F/P AND
CASTLEMAN ⊕s

A349

MEADOWS

1·1

97

MERLEY HALL FARM TO LAKE GATES

Keep straight on past the house and the low, brick-buttressed barn at the RH side of the road and around a sweeping bend with a deep ditch and hedge on your left and elevated cottages on your right.   The next gate on your right leads into fields behind the high hedge whilst, past a couple more house on your left, Ashington Lane turns off past a paddock - to Ashington.

A Stour Valley Way (SVW from now on) arrow by the Willett Road sign confirms that you keep straight on along the lane.   On a sweeping right bend in the road, the right verge widens out and a ditch appears on your left.

After Lake Farm Cottage and the Lake Farm buildings, the ditch over on your left disappears and the lane soon acquires a pavement instead.   Walk on the pavement to the end of Willett Road and then cross over to the RH corner where another pavement with a deep verge turns right along Wimborne Road as it comes down from Corfe Mullen to your left.

Follow the Wimborne Road pavement down to the Wimborne By-Pass roundabout and take care - it's a very busy road.   Cross over the By-Pass to the far corner.

Turn left to cross Julians Road and double back a little to find the SVW signpost lurking on a steep slope in the wide verge.   Drop down to the footpath-arrowed stile and climb over (I hope it isn't very boggy this time) and don't cross any of the drainage ditches.   Work your way through the fences and stiles, however they may be placed.   They seem to change at various times.

You need to bear right and follow the top of a hawthorn-bedecked bank until you have passed a gate in the road fence over on your right.   Now, turn down the bank between two hawthorns and aim to the right of a pair of old willows - one with a huge hanging branch (unless it's fallen off now).   Here you will find a Footpath-arrowed bridge and a stile.   Go over the stile into a long, wide level field and stop.

Important Instructions:

You want to turn sharp right along the wire fence to find the way across this vast open field but there is often a very wet area in your way so, what I do is walk straight ahead from the bridge for 50 yards and then turn at right angles.

From here, you will see a gap in the hawthorns about 200 yards away - 50 yards to the left of the only oak tree (334 degrees for the technical.   Straight at the skyline pylon without the white cottages below it for the non-technical).   Now turn to Stage 4 where you will be joining walkers from Route 2 at Eye Bridge.

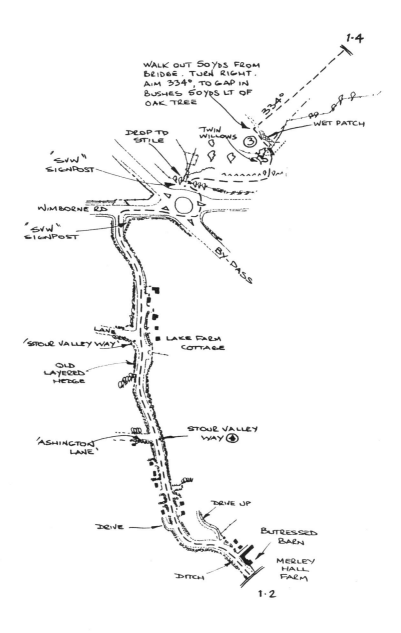

1·4

WALK OUT 50 YDS FROM
BRIDGE. TURN RIGHT.
AIM 334°, TO GAP IN
BUSHES 50 YDS LT OF
OAK TREE

334°

WET PATCH

TWIN
WILLOWS ③

DROP TO
STILE

"SVW"
SIGNPOST

WIMBORNE RD

"SVW"
SIGNPOST

BY-PASS

LANE

LAKE FARM
COTTAGE

"STOUR VALLEY WAY"

OLD
LAYERED
HEDGE

STOUR VALLEY
WAY ④

"ASHINGTON
LANE"

DRIVE UP

BUTRESSED
BARN

DRIVE

MERLEY
HALL
FARM

DITCH

1·2

ROUTE 1 - STAGE 4

LAKE GATES AND/OR EYE BRIDGE TO COWGROVE

ROUTE 1: Approaching the gap, you will see a stile on the other side with 3 cottages as a distant background.   On arrival at the aforementioned gap, 50 yds from the oak tree, cross the ditch and bear slightly left towards the stile in the wire fence facing you.   A second ditch crosses your path before the stile.   Over the stile, follow a due-North path across the next vast field, aiming for a single hawthorn bush and the wire fence corner post.   Aim for the highest cottage on the hill ahead (the only one without a thatched roof).   At the corner post, you will find footpath and a SVW arrows.   Now, choose a route which takes you steadily away from the wire fence (18 degrees from North) towards the far distant end of the long, narrowing field.   In the far corner, you will find a stile with a footpath arrow.   Go over and follow the LH wire fence to the steps up onto Eye Bridge. Go up onto the bridge.   Now, read **'All together'**.

ROUTE 2: Are you up on the bridge.   You should be.   Read **'All together'**.

ALL TOGETHER: From up here, there are superb views along the River Stour to Wimborne.   The Roman ford is clearly visible and is still in use (by tractors). Leaving the bridge, you have a choice of paths to Cowgrove.   Both ways have their own merits.   The road way affords good views over the Stour valley as it passes the National Trust's Old Court House and some lovely thatched cottages. But of course, the riverside path gives a superb close-up of Dorset's loveliest river.   Now, follow one of the following:

A. THE RIVER PATH: Come down off the bridge and go over the N.T.-arrowed stile on its right, upstream side.   Follow the wide grassy path between the RH wire fence and the tree-clad bank of the meandering River Stour.   Keep an eye open for kingfishers and herons - you'll see neither unless you're absolutely silent.   After a bridge and stile, the river has deposited a growing island on this side whilst it is still undercutting on the outer sweeps of its bends. Over the next stile, next to a gate, three paths present themselves.   Turn right and follow the edge of the wire fence with the second path below you.   A few zig-zags follow the fence until, at a footbridge across a ditch, you should descend and join the lower path which is less boggy from here on.   After a 'Private' gate, the path bends round to the left to another stile which leads out onto Cowgrove Common.   Follow the RH hedge around to cross a ditch by a small bridge and follow the path past a footpath sign.   Cross Cowgrove road and walk past the left end of three poplars. Pass a duckpond and bear left onto a gravel track past Poplar Farm.

B. THE ROAD PATH: Leaving the car park, turn left onto the road.   Keep straight on past the two right turnings and the low hedge allows good views over the lush River valley farmland.   After the recently restored Old Court House and Lower Dairy Cottage on your left and Walnut Farm on your right, you pass the barns of the Old Lower Dairy.   Next to the Firs Farmhouse, there is a rare grain store supported by rat-defeating staddle stones.   It's good to see them being used for their original purpose.   In a few more yards, you reach Cowgrove Common where a footpath arrow points left past the thatched Drews Cottage. Bear off to the right here, past three tall poplars and onto the gravel track which runs between the duckpond and Poplar Farm.

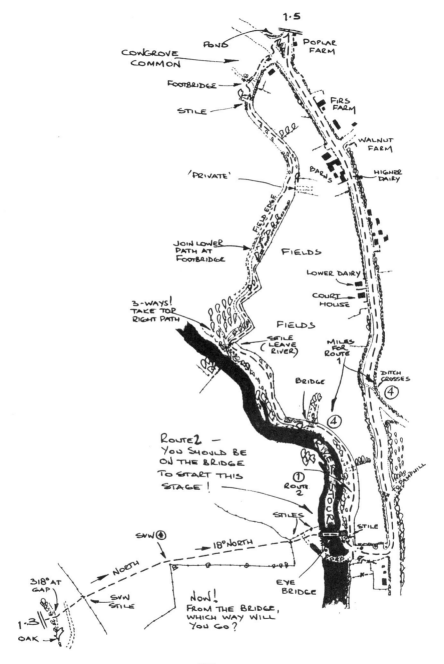

1·5

POND

COWGROVE
COMMON

POPLAR
FARM

FOOTBRIDGE

FIRS
FARM

STILE

WALNUT
FARM

'PRIVATE'

BARNS

HIGHER
DAIRY

FIELD EDGE

JOIN LOWER
PATH AT
FOOTBRIDGE

FIELDS

LOWER DAIRY

COURT
HOUSE

3-WAYS!
TAKE TOP
RIGHT PATH

FIELDS

STILE
(LEAVE
RIVER)

MILES
FOR
ROUTE
1

DITCH
CROSSES

④

BRIDGE

④

ROUTE 2 —
YOU SHOULD BE
ON THE BRIDGE
TO START THIS
STAGE!

①
ROUTE
2

PARDHILL

STILES

STILE

SVW ④

18° NORTH

NORTH

STILE

FORD

318° AT
GAP

SVW
STILE

EYE
BRIDGE

1·3

OAK

NOW!
FROM THE BRIDGE,
WHICH WAY WILL
YOU GO?

ROUTE 1 - STAGE 5

COWGROVE TO PAMPHILL SCHOOL

Past the pond, go past a steel barrier and footpath and Bridleway arrows onto the bending track. With hedges and fences on either side, the first LH bend goes around a smaller pond and the gravel track then bears back to the right past an old willow and a thatched cottage. Still meandering, the track comes into Little Cowgrove Common with a stile in the far right, wire fence. Keep straight on with the ditch and hedge on your left opening out into the common.

A few yards further, you pass the red brick No.1 New Road and, just before the track joins another tarmac lane, turn sharp right just past this cottage. A SVW signpost on the edge of the common points up the narrow track to 'Pamphill 1' whilst the original signpost confirms that the track is 'All Fools Lane'.

This is a lovely, shady stroll up a really ancient hollow-way, confirmed by its great depth in the steeper parts and its collection of ancient oaks. In a few yards, cross George's Crossing by two 1/2 gates and enjoy the gentle uphill walk. Seasonally, harts tongue ferns, bluebells and common ferns fill much of the bank as you continue upwards. After a lofty pylon towers above a particularly deep section of the gully, wooden steps and a footbridge carry you up and over a ditch with masses of bluebells to your right and a lower field on your left. Keep straight on up, past hollies and a couple of really old oaks until the sides become progressively lower. Another gated crossing allows glimpses of an old wood to your left from where loud bird song can usually be heard.

Suddenly, the track levels out with a ditch on your right and you pass a thatched cottage on the LH hedged corner to emerge onto Abbot Street with the wooded edge of Kingston Lacy Park over the opposite bank. A SVW signpost on the corner points to 'Pamphill 1/2' whilst the left turning takes you down to the Old Forge. Turn right along Abbot Street, past the wooded corner and a gateway. *The road continues past the white-painted iron railings of St Stephen's Church to Pamphill Dairy Farm Shop and Tea Rooms. Both places are well worth a visit for spiritual and bodily comfort - in that order.* The next part of the route turns right off the road here, between low wooden posts onto a path which meanders past a RH hedge to a small bridge over a ditch which deposits you into the National Trust car park for 'Pamphill Green'. *From the car park, two tracks go to the right. The first heads to a 17thC cottage whilst the second goes to Pamphill Manor House. This was built in the 17thC by Matthew Bentall, steward to Sir Ralph Bankes, the builder of Kingston Lacy House.*

Follow the line of The Oak Avenue. *It was planted in 1846 and you are ambling across seven centuries of history because this village green dates back to the 13thC. It is a Registered Village Green and enjoys the full protection of the Law. If there is no cricket being played, you might as well keep going, but not without noticing the fine thatched pavilion which was built in 1909.*

At the end of the avenue, go past the anti-car barrier and an array of gates on the right and keep following the road to the brick building with a postbox on its LH corner for your postcards home.

102

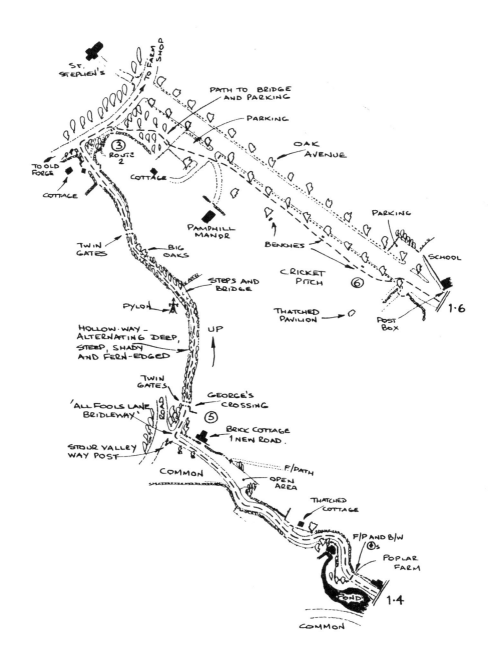

ROUTE 1 - STAGE 6

PAMPHILL SCHOOL TO STOUR PATH

Pamphill almshouses and Free Writing School were founded in 1698 by Roger Gillingham of the Middle Temple. The central part is now Pamphill First School. Keep on down the road, past a pair of footpath arrows by a ditch on the RH corner of the common. After a LH SVW arrow and a clump of trees and bushes and the RH National Trust 'Little Pamphill Green' sign, you reach a grassy clearing on your left. Just before the hedged garden of the first cottage, walk onto the clearing past a 'Wimborne 1.1/4' sign and, ignoring all of the green tracks which return to the First School, wander underneath the spreading legs of an electricity pylon. Look up - these pylons are even bigger than you think when one's towering above your head. Circumnavigating just the one leg, bear right and drop down between the bushes, past the NT footpath arrow, onto the sloping valley sides.

A gravel path leads you in a serpentine way down to a stile with a bulkily-enclosed area on its left. You could safely watch some seriously fierce wildlife from within its barricade. Over the stile, follow the path circuitously down to some railed steps. At the foot of the steps, ignore all paths except the one which turns right and follows a row of trees astride a fenced scarp with the valley floor below it. For your assistance, it is signposted 'Nature Walk'.

Along the level path with tree-clad slopes to your right, you will reach another stile with SVW arrows. Go over the stile and down the steps into the valley floor with an array of bluebells if the time is right. Cross the level floor to a single hand-railed bridge across a small stream and a stile on the other bank. Over the stile, turn right at a SVW post and follow the bottom fence, hedge and stream along the grassy side of the valley. As you follow the field (no path visible), the stream and fence change sides a couple of times. Your route takes you through two ditches and over an intriguing bank which continues along a line formed by trees which stand in a regimented line up the LH slope.

The stream leaves the field by running under the RH hedge into the road from Pamphill and the Vine Inn. At the end of the field, go over the stile between a gate and an electricity post. The road outside warns you to go 'Slow' as you turn right for a few yards until you find the SVW-arrowed stile in the LH hedge. Vine Hill is on your right as you reach the stile. Go over the stile into the level field beyond where - lo and behold - there is the stream again over against the LH hedge. Follow the hedge towards the River Stour.

In about 100 yards, you will find a footbridge and a stile where another SVW sign advises it is only 1/2 mile to Wimborne. Over the bridge and stile by the big old willow tree, cross the next field and enjoy the level grassy stroll along the edge of the River Stour. The next stile boasts an even bigger willow with its branches dropping gracefully into the River. Cross this footbridge and ignore the path which runs away to your left. Keep straight on alongside a couple of short sections of wire fence.

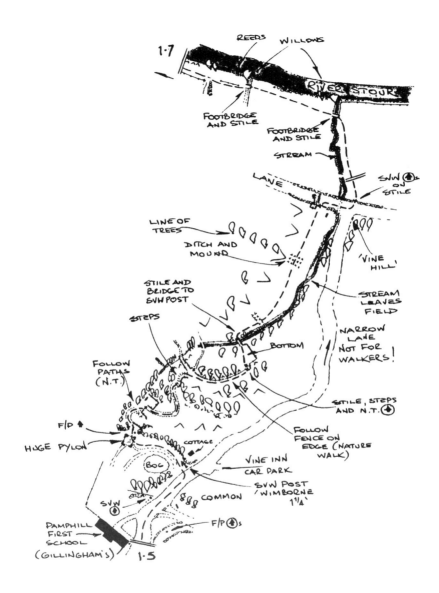

ROUTE 1 - STAGE 7

STOUR PATH TO WIMBORNE

Keep straight on past the football pitches on your left and past a water outfall. Between hawthorns and some small trees, you enter an area of allotments with a track coming from your left. Aim straight on, towards the visible Minster until you reach the end of the allotments to find a footpath sign pointing back to Eye Bridge. Joining a tarmac road (Old Road) with a block of flats to your right, follow the road around to your left, between townhouses and garages until you reach a Pay and Display car park on the corner of Old Road.

Cross Victoria Road and turn right to the junction with King Street, West Street and Julians Road. Turn left at the Pudding and Pye into West Street.

Keep straight on along West Street until it bends to the left on its way to The Square and the Kings Head Hotel Turn right into West Row and you will see the old Wesleyan Chapel facing you. Bear left and right past the Chapel and you arrive in Cornmarket with the White Hart Inn on your right and the Oddfellows Hall along the paved courtyard to your left. Walk across to Cooks Row and turn into the Minster or keep straight on to find your start point at the Tourist Information Centre and the Priest's House Museum. *If you haven't got time today, you really must come back and explore Wimborne another time. There is plenty to see and enjoy here. Tourist Information will tell you everything you need to know.*

Roger Gillingham's Almshouses, Pamphill - Page 104

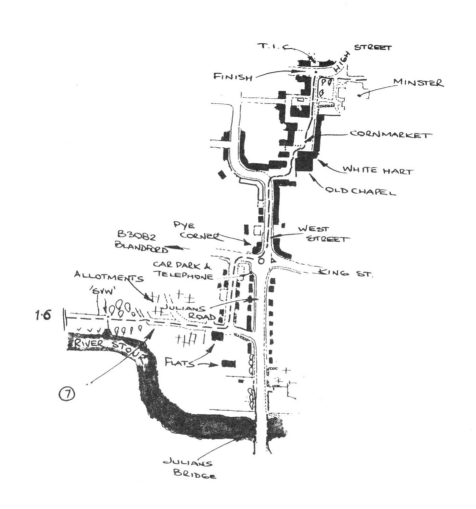

ROUTE 2 - STAGE 1

WIMBORNE TO EYE BRIDGE

From outside the Tourist Information Centre, cross over High Street into Cooks Row.   The Minster Church of St. Cuthburga is on your left and, as you pass, look over to a high window in the North wall.   *The chap in the red jacket is the Quarter Jack.   He has been dressed as a Grenadier since the Napoleonic wars but, when he was carved in 1613, he wore a monks habit.   He rings the quarter hours.* Now, walk up to Cornmarket and pass the White Hart as you leave in the far corner.   Follow the lane past the old chapel and out into West Street.   Cross over and walk up to the junction with Victoria Road (the B3082 to Blandford Forum) with the Pudding and Pye on the corner.

Go around the corner and cross over into Old Road with a Pay and Display car park on your left and the Green Man Inn over on your right.   Walk all the way along Old Road and turn right at the end.   Keep straight on past the two blocks of flats in Cuthbury Close and into a large area of allotments.   Follow the track straight on through the allotments - with the River Stour joining you on the left.

After Wimborne Town F.C. football ground on your right, keep following the riverside path, first one side of a wire fence and then on the other until you reach a bridge over a ditch with a stile on the far side.   There is a large willow next to it. Keep straight on to another bridge, stile and willow.

On the other side, look to your right and you will see a stile in the far hedge.   This is for information only because that is where you will be coming back after your journey around Cowgrove and Pamphill.

Now, follow the path slightly away from the river's edge, aiming for a stile by the gate in the wire fence ahead of you.   Over the stile, there is a pretty cottage on your right.   Cross this short field to another stile by a gate.   Climb over and turn left through the little car park and note where a barrier stops accidental plunges into the river where the Roman ford is still in use by tractors.

Walk round to the right and go up onto Eye Bridge.   Here is where you join the Route 1 walkers who are coming across the meadows on the other side of the bridge along what was once a Roman road from Moriconium (now Hamworthy) to Badbury Rings.

All you have to decide now is whether to follow the river to Cowgrove or to use the road instead.   Turn to Stage 1.4 before you decide.   That's right 1.4.   You're all on the same Stage Maps from here on.

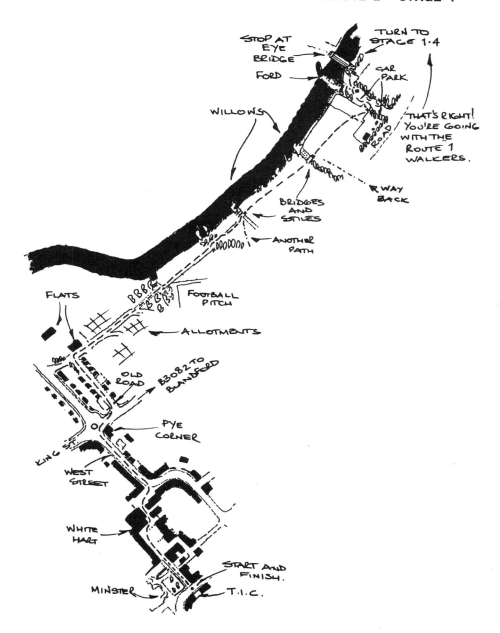

PART EIGHT - BERE REGIS

INTRODUCTION

In common with many people who tend not to notice the beauty in familiar surroundings, I seem to have neglected this lovely part of Dorset although it is only twenty minutes away from home.   Although I had often been caught in traffic jams at the old town traffic lights before the coming of the by-pass, I never explored Bere Regis itself.   Now that it is so quiet, it's a joy to wander around and admire the cottages and houses and to visit the jewel in the crown of Bere Regis - The Church of St John the Baptist.   Viewed from Woodbury Hill, the town appears to lie in a bowl of green patchwork.   The Church tower and the fine Old Vicarage show proudly above the clay tiled roofs all around.   Bere Regis stands on the North edge of the Great Heath which stretches from Poole to Dorchester. The land to the South of the town is covered by the heather and bracken of the Great Heath with its tiny villages and wild landscapes.   There are chalk downs, grass and gravel paths, woodland birds and country crows to keep you company - and there is always an excellent chance of seeing wild deer.

THE ALTERNATIVES

All three walks begin and end in West Street at the junction with Manor Farm Road (only because it's handy for the car park and the bus stop) - at Reference SY846949 on O S Map No. 194.   There are several buses stopping in Bere Regis including the Wilts and Dorset 186-189 inclusive and the local 312 and 316.

ROUTE 1: Total distance 9.1/4 miles.   This Route takes you onto the Great Heath and visits some typical Piddle valley villages with thatched cob and timber cottages and the strange Culpepper's Dish.   Ancient hollow-ways lead through the high downs and into Turners Puddle with its tiny abandoned church.   Then there is pretty Briantspuddle.   Several footbridges cross the River Piddle whilst mixed woodland walks lead through the high country with lovely views all around.

ROUTE 2: Total distance 3.1/4 miles.   This Route takes you up through the woods of Black Hill and onto the Great Heath to sample its delights but then it makes a quick return to join all the other Routes for the last mile into Bere Regis.

ROUTE 3: Total distance 6 miles.   Although it misses the fine views from the Ridgeway woods, the spectacle of Culpepper's Dish and the lovely village of Briantspuddle, this shorter Route gives you the chance of a thought-provoking walk along part of the medieval road which once thronged with travellers between Dorchester and the port of Wareham - and, before them, the barrow builders of the Stone and Bronze ages.

STAGE	MILES	TOTAL MILES
ROUTE 1:		
1 Bere Regis to Black Hill	1	1
2 Black Hill to Turners Puddle	.75	1.75

STAGE	MILES	TOTAL MILES
ROUTE 1 CONTINUED:		
3 Turners Puddle to Throop	1	2.75
4 Throop to Ridgeway Wood	1	3.75
5 Ridgeway Wood to Tolpuddle Road	1.50	5.25
6 Tolpuddle Road to Piddle Wood	1.75	7
7 Piddle Wood to Shitterton	1.25	8.25
8 Shitterton to Southbrook	.50	8.75
1 Southbrook to Bere Regis	.50	**9.25**
ROUTE 2:		
1 Bere Regis to Black Hill	1.75	1.75
7 Black Hill to Shitterton	.50	2.25
8 Shitterton to Southbrook	.50	2.75
1 Southbrook to Bere Regis	.50	**3.25**
ROUTE 3:		
1 Bere Regis to Black Hill	1	1
2 Black Hill to Turners Puddle	.75	1.75
3 Through Turners Puddle	1	2.75
6 Turners Puddle to Piddle Wood	1	3.75
7 Piddle Wood to Shitterton	1.25	5
8 Shitterton to Southbrook	.50	5.50
1 Southbrook to Bere Regis	.50	**6**

ROUTE LAYOUT

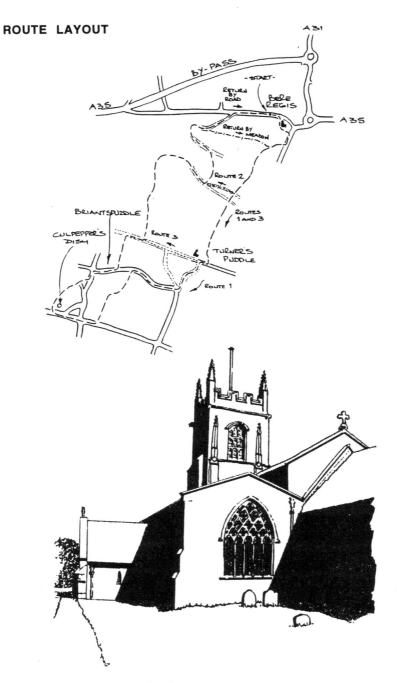

St John the Baptist, Bere Regis

Church of the Holy Trinity, Turner's Puddle. Page 118

Looking back through Briantspuddle - Page 122

STAGE 1

BERE REGIS TO BLACK HILL and SOUTHBROOK TO BERE REGIS

OUTWARD ROUTES: Starting in the middle of West Street with the bus stop on your left and Manor Farm Road leading to the car park on your right, head due East. Past the Stores, the Drax Arms and the Old Vicarage up the drive on your left, turn down Church Lane on your right and follow it down, past the new vicarage, to the twin gates which lead into the churchyard of St John the Baptist's. You'll find a few details about this wonderful church at the end of Stage 8. Go straight past the East Chancel and bear left on the path towards the twin gates and kissing gate. You will find yourself in a wide tarmac drive between a walled garden of cottages on your left and a house on the right. Walk down to find the pavement of the Bere Regis to Wool road.

In the field opposite, you will see the half brick and half stone West end of a fine farmhouse. *This is the L-shaped Court Farm, the oldest part of which is the late 17thC or early 18thC stone part which is facing you. Here once stood a great manor house where Queen Elfrida (or Ethelfreda) retired, as Sir Frederick Treves says, "haunted and remorseful after the murder of her stepson Edward at Corfe Castle" in 978AD. King John, brother of Richard, had a hunting base here and, in Henry III's time, the manor was held by Simon de Montfort, Earl of Leicester. It came to Robert Turberville in the reign of Henry VIII and it remained in their hands for three hundred years. The first of this distinguished family to arrive in England was Sir Payne de Turberville who came with William the Conqueror, but it was nearly five hundred years before they settled in Bere.*

Now, walk to the right, away from Bere Regis to cross Elder Road and the Bere stream as it runs away to join the River Piddle and Poole Harbour. Past the watercress beds on either side of the road, turn right into 'Southbrook, leading to Egdon Close'. Follow the lane around the bends, with houses up on your left and the watercress beds down on your right, past a Footpath-arrowed stile. *This is the stile where all of the Routes come back into Bere Regis.* When you see the cemetery gates, head on up the hill and join the unsigned Bridleway which runs between the cemetery iron railed wall on your left and the houses on the right.

This hollow-way is filled with harts-tongue ferns. Edged with a smattering of coppiced hazels and old oaks, the track ascends and becomes flinty underfoot where the downward-rushing rainwater has scoured away the path. The sides are higher as the path grows steeper but, as you reach a short level part, the sides are quite low with fields and fine views on both sides. After a descending, unsigned, Bridleway on your right, the track goes up to a LH stile and a gate across your path. Ignore the stile! Go through the gate into the oak and coppiced wood which signals the start of your journey onto the Great Heath. Stop to find your direction. It's practically straight on up the hill, to the right of the two biggest oaks ahead of you. For the technical, take a bearing of 210º and aim for one of two sets of tree root steps in front of you.

RETURN ROUTES: Reaching the stile at the far end of the meadow, you'll find yourself back in Southbrook so just walk back into the town and you've finished. Well done!

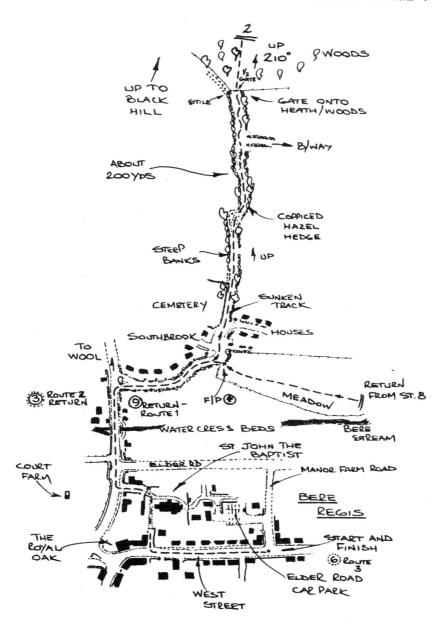

STAGE 2

BLACK HILL TO TURNERS PUDDLE

Both of these paths meet in 20 yards' time so it doesn't matter which one you choose. From here, the path is narrow and it wavers from West to South West. There will be glimpses of Bere Regis far down on your right as your path becomes narrow and sandy. As you pass between a pair of short silver birches, you meet the first crop of gorse bushes on the poor soil of the Great Heath.

The Great Heath is mostly built on the gravel of Reading and Bagshot beds whilst this first part is still a thin cap of gravel over a chalk base. All over the heath, the top soil consists mostly of thin, broken-down heather and bracken. There isn't much for trees to live on and any rainwater soon soaks down through the chalk or gravel beneath. This is a land of short, struggling trees and bushes amongst an array of gorse, bracken and heather. The trees are mostly birches and holly with a few poor oaks scattered about.

Keep following the narrow path. There is a group of six bell and bowl-barrows here on the boundary between the parishes of Bere Regis and Turners Puddle. The heath is covered in plants which produce a seasonal array of flowers, including primroses, foxgloves, the gorse and the heather. With the fine views and the song of skylarks and yellow-hammers, this is a beautiful place to be.

Now, with gorse and bracken all around, the terrain becomes more level but with a shallow valley over on your left. Keep following the path, grassier at the edges now, between a fat, round holly bush on the right and a medium-sized oak on the left. The path then opens out as it meets a crossing gravel track with grass up the middle.

ROUTE 2: *If you only want a short walk, turn right on this gravel track. Follow this Stage map and it will lead you to the return path for a very pleasant walk of only 4 miles in total. Then, to continue, turn to Stage 7.*

THE REST: A wire fence over on the left borders a working gravel pit but this won't bother us. Cross over the track, and keep straight on (SW) through gorse and past two short spruce trees. The gravel pit fence is still over on the left as the narrower path passes between another RH oak near a depression/hole and a LH holly bush. There is an interesting 'erratic' rock on the left bank before the path meets another crossing gravel track. *(Here is another chance to make a short cut on Route 2).* Zig-zag slightly left/right to cross over into a descending flint and gravel path down (SW) through gorse and heather.

Follow the winding track down into a sparse wood of holly and oak trees. On a left bend, a huge old oak with branches overhanging your path carries Bridleway and Footpath arrows. Keep to the track, straight down the widening gully, past a crossing of unsigned and faint paths, until you reach a Bridleway-arrowed gate which leads out of the woods and into a steep-sided track with ferns in the banks. You are leaving the heath for the moment and rejoining farmland that was hard-won from the heather, the gorse, the bracken and the gravel which is never far below your feet. This hedged and grassy hollow-way descends between fields for 1/4 mile so just enjoy yourself on the downhill, comfortable stroll.

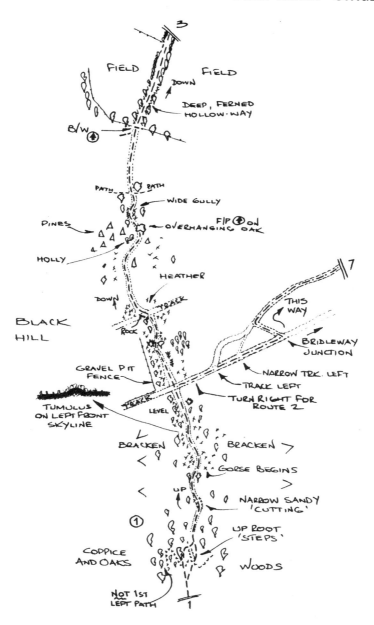

FIELD

FIELD

3

DOWN

DEEP, FERNED
HOLLOW·WAY

B/W

PATH — PATH

WIDE GULLY

PINES

F/P ON
OVERHANGING OAK

HOLLY

HEATHER

DOWN

TRACK

7

THIS
WAY

BLACK
HILL

ROCK

BRIDLEWAY
JUNCTION

GRAVEL PIT
FENCE

NARROW TRK. LEFT

TRACK LEFT

TRACK

LEVEL

TURN RIGHT FOR
ROUTE 2

TUMULUS
ON LEFT FRONT
SKYLINE

BRACKEN

BRACKEN

GORSE BEGINS

UP

NARROW SANDY
'CUTTING'

1

UP ROOT
'STEPS'

COPPICE
AND OAKS

WOODS

NOT 1ST
LEFT PATH

1

117

TURNERS PUDDLE TO THROOP

The bottom gate leads into Toner's Puddle Farm but don't go through. Turn left before the gate and follow the signed, grassy Bridleway around the left edge of the barn yard. Through the half-gate and past a Bridleway signpost, turn right onto the road.

Just to your left, you will see a line of short, pollarded willows which mark the line of a tributary of the River Piddle. This was originally a man-made irrigation channel for the water meadows. *The road which you are treading was once the main road from the port of Wareham to Tolpuddle and Dorchester, following the North side of the river. In medieval times, Wareham was the major port but, when the river and the West side of Poole Harbour silted up (and the ships got bigger), Poole took over the role. Two sluggish rivers run into Wareham - The Frome and the Piddle - and, over hundreds of years, silting up of the estuary became inevitable. The major result of this, as far as our journey is concerned, is that this road fell into disuse and the turnpike road which runs from Dorchester to Poole (now the A35) came into being.* Here, the road changes to a Bridleway until it reduces still further to a Footpath 1.1/2 miles before Tolpuddle.

Walk straight on past the farm buildings on your right and past a signed turning 'Bridleway. Throop 1/3' between a wood-fenced paddock and an old oak wood on your left. Just past this turn, you will find the Church of the Holy Trinity, Turners Puddle. *Sir Frederick Treves, in his "Highways and Byways of Dorset" of 1906, called this church "pathetically plain...and...childlike". Built about 1500, it was badly damaged in a storm of 1758. The top of the West tower was rebuilt in 1760 and a Victorian restoration took place in 1859. The corrugated asbestos roof appeared in the early 1960's to make the building waterproof.*

These Puddle villages are listed together as Pidele in the Domesday Book and this little hamlet had 40 goats and 12 mares with their foals. This present hamlet's name is derived from later owners of the manor. Henry Tonere was a knight in the reign of Edward I (1272-1307) who "held one knight's fee in Piddle Tonere" in 1297 and fought against the Scots at Berwick-upon-Tweed in 1302.

ROUTE 3: Keep straight on past the church - signed 'Bridleway. Tolpuddle 2'. Then turn to Stage 6.

ROUTE 1: After visiting the church, and snatching a glimpse of the 16th-18thC Tonerspuddle Farmhouse next door, go back to the Throop Bridleway and cross the footbridge over the tributary, next to the ford. Follow the winding, gravel and grass track. Another bridge crosses the River Piddle and the track continues past a thatched cottage and a left Footpath to 'Brockhill 1/2'. Your road, for such it once was, runs South of the River Piddle to Affpuddle.

Leaving the Bridleway, you emerge into Throop with lovely thatched cottages on either side of the road to your left. Keep straight on, past Throop House on your left and the Bridleway track to 'Kite Hill 1/2' over the River Piddle on your right. Keep following the road for 1/4 mile with a hedged bank on the left and hedged and fenced meadows on your right.

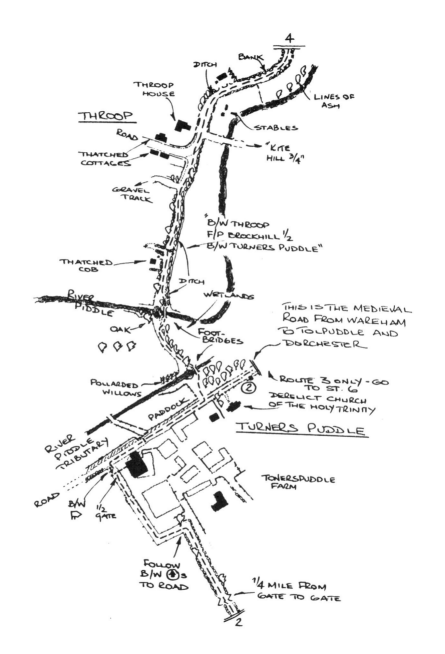

STAGE 4

THROOP TO RIDGEWAY WOOD

You may have noticed that a line of trees shows the route of the River Piddle over on your right. *Quite recklessly, I pointed these out on the last Stage Map as ash trees. However, due to my continuing blind-spot in the realms of tree identification in winter, they may have been hornbeams. The problem is that, in winter, both of these trees have bunches of hanging seed-pods similar to the wings of sycamore helicopters but single. Both have rough barks and, if they don't have piles of dead leaves lying on the ground to show whether they have long, toothed leaves like hornbeams or sets of leaves on either side of a long stalk like the ash, I'm still unable to tell them apart. I have no doubt that you will find me in error about this as you pass along some of my routes but, if you do, you are probably much warmer than I was when I planned and checked this particular walk in the crisp, finger-blueing air of January and February.*

Keep going along the sunken road, passing a verge and a ditch on your right. After a big oak on the left, a gravel track turns left into a field opposite a farm gate in the right fence. After another big oak, turn left by a Wessex Water station, signposted 'Footpath. Morton 2.1/2'. Past the gate to Meadow Cottage, go over a stile with a Footpath arrow and join the gravel track as it runs, between wire fences, up towards a high deciduous wood. After the hedged and walled gardens of a long, low building with pillars and a Chinese-hatted gateway on your right, go through a gateway or over a stile into a gravel barnyard. Keep straight on uphill to where the track turns left. Leave the track at the bend and cross a grassy bridge over the ditch to a Footpath-arrowed stile. Climb over into the old oak wood and follow the rough footpath around to the right to cross a sleeper bridge. Turn left to follow the path uphill before crossing another sleeper bridge and turning left and following the fence. At the top of the woods, you pass a high wire-fenced enclosure on the left and arrive at a stile with a Footpath arrow on one of the posts.

Over this stile, you are in a big field which slopes down to a valley on your left. Look for the stile at the far side of this field, leading into the dark pine wood at the top. Aim past the two stunted bushes in front of you - 240º South West - looking for the yellow dot on the distant post.

On the way up the field, there are superb views back to Black Hill and the hills and fields beyond. At the stile, you will notice that the pine wood is fringed with old oaks. There appear to be defensive earth banks within the woods but, apparently, they're quite natural. Go over the stile and bear a little right to go over an earth bank onto a pine needle-covered forest track up through the dismal, dark and dead wood. If the light-masking trees have been felled, as they must be soon, enjoy the sky. It hasn't been visible for years from this track.

Ignore a right-forking track and keep on up to find a wide, grassy margin between the top edge of the woods and the Ridgeway road. Pass through the bracken, gorse and blackberry bushes onto the high road where a confirmation Footpath arrow points back into the woods for 'Briantspuddle 1/2' and across the road to an arrowed tree for 'Morton 2'. Turn right and walk along the road. *Watch out for tourists meandering along the road in their cars looking for Culpepper's Dish.*

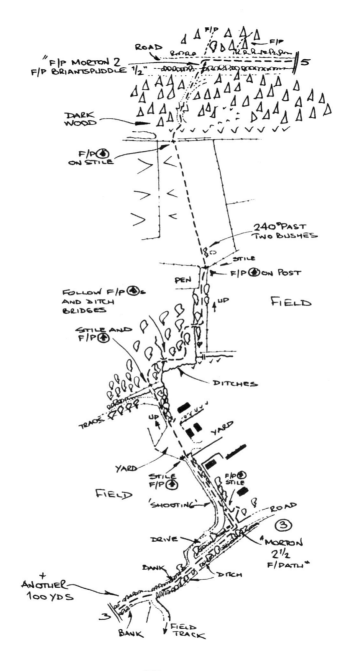

"F/P MORTON 2
F/P BRIANTSPUDDLE ½"

ROAD

F/P

F/P

5

DARK
WOOD

F/P ● ON STILE

240° PAST
TWO BUSHES

STILE

F/P ● ON POST

PEN

FOLLOW F/P ● s
AND DITCH
BRIDGES

FIELD

STILE AND
F/P ●

UP

DITCHES

TRACK

UP

YARD

YARD

STILE
F/P ●

FIELD

F/P ●
STILE

'SHOOTING'

ROAD

③

DRIVE

"MORTON
2½
F/PATH"

BANK

DITCH

+
ANOTHER
100 YDS

3

BANK

FIELD
TRACK

STAGE 5

RIDGEWAY WOOD TO TOLPUDDLE ROAD

Along the level road through the mixed pine and deciduous woods, cross over the junction with the Bovington to Affpuddle road and keep straight on. A Bridleway forest track turns off to the left alongside a deep depression in the ground, cloaked in trees and with trees growing in the bottom. *This is a smaller version of Culpepper's Dish known as Culpepper's Spoon.* Keep on up the gorse-edged road and you'll soon arrive at the 'Culpepper's Dish Car Park'. *There are several choices for the spelling such as Culpeper and Cull-Pepper, which you meet in a minute or two, but I prefer this one, as spelt by the famous herbalist in question.*

Before going on, walk across to the far right of the car park where a wide gap in the pines allows fine views over the Heath, from the South to the South West, towards the coastal ridges between Lulworth and Weymouth. Now return to the road and look through the bracken and brambles to see the amazing depths of the 100 yards diameter Culpepper's Dish proper. *If that is only 40ft deep......I'm really quite surprised. These holes are the result of subterranean streams tapping a layer of sand and gravel and, like holes in the sand on the beach, the sand is pulled down into the hole by the subsidence at the very bottom.*

Take refuge in the faint parallel grass track against the woods on this side of the road and walk on for about 100 yards. There is a fingerpost for 'Briantspuddle 1/3' on the left side of the road pointing to a track into the mixed pine and beech woods. There is also a Bridleway arrow on the first tree. Turn down the path and follow it for 200 yards down and up to a wide gravel forest track with a three-way Bridleway finger-post. Ignore the wide grass track opposite and turn right onto the level gravel track, signed 'Bridleway. Briantspuddle 1/4'.

Around the first bend, the forest track comes onto your route from the left then bends round and descends to the right. However, keep straight on, onto the narrower track, signed 'Bridleway. Briantspuddle'. There is an 8ft (2.5m) drop on your right. After two grass tracks have turned off to the left, your path begins to descend with a hanging beech wood on your left. More assorted arrows and side tracks bring you down to find a thatched cottage behind a beech hedge in front of you. Turn left at the cottage and follow its hedge down and around to the right.

Follow the gravel track down, between high banks with harts-tongue ferns, to a tarmac road at the bottom with a very high bank with oaks and ferns facing you. Turn left and follow the road down, past an old cottage high up on your left, into the pretty Briantspuddle village. Turn right at the cross-roads, signed 'Throop 3/4', with Bladen Valley to your left and Bere Regis straight on. Enjoy a stroll between some lovely thatched cottages and past Bladen Social Club and Village Hall on your left. *Note the Youth Club on brick arches - to let the flooding river in and out?* Just before the second turning circle on the right, with larger cottages around it, turn left before a bungalow at the 'Footpath. Gully Road 1/4' sign.

Climb over the Footpath-arrowed stile by the gate into the long meadow beyond and walk over to the footbridge. Cross the stepped bridge over the River Piddle and cross the field to the gate, over the Piddle tributary and onto the medieval Tolpuddle road. Turn right, signposted 'Bridleway Turners Puddle 1/2'.

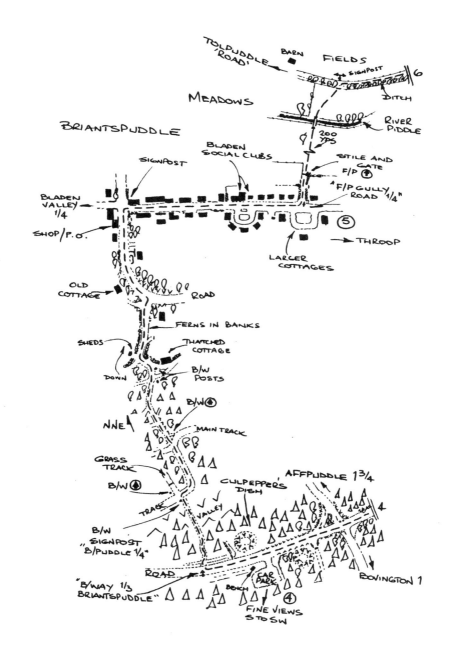

STAGE 6

TOLPUDDLE ROAD TO PIDDLE WOOD

ROUTE 1: Follow the Bridleway/track between the LH wire fenced fields and the RH hedged stream.   After 1/4 mile, the track widens out at a farm gate on the left.   A large oak stands on the facing corner and a Bridleway sign points up the left track to 'Kite Hill 1/2' whilst the straight-on track returns to 'Turners Puddle 1/3'.   *'Thirds' are a little unusual.*   Turn left onto the track in the rising field.

ROUTE 3: After the twin white gates on your right, the small wood between your track and the tributary of the River Piddle ends.   Follow the level track with fenced fields on either side, passing a gated track into one of the RH fields and a signposted Bridleway over the stream which leads to 'Throop 1/4'.   Just a few yards after this turning, when you reach a large oak on the near RH corner of a right turn into a gated field, signposted 'Bridleway. Kite Hill 1/4', turn right onto the rising track.   The Bridleway straight on continues the medieval road towards 'Tolpuddle 1.2/3'

ROUTES 1 AND 3: Walk up the curving track.   There are good views along the low river valley on your right and, beyond there, you will see the Heath re-appearing on the distant ridge.   Nearly 1/2 mile later, your track bears left into a thicket of hawthorn and pines whilst a right branch turns down to an old chalk-pit .

There are superb views back to the coastal ridge behind you as the gravel track begins to follow the East edge of the high pines and coppiced hazel wood.   The wide fields to your right allow far views to the Heath and beyond.   After a short descent, the gravel track bends left and begins to climb between pines and coppice.   Keep straight on to a sharp left bend with a grass track going straight on.   Keep to the main track and, over the next 100 yards, the track descends and ascends across a more open area of mixed trees.

As you climb the last few yards, there is sky straight ahead indicating the edge of a ridge.   The trees cloaking the Northern slopes are mostly old oaks and, turning right onto the track, your ascending route runs between old hazel coppices.   A gully on your left indicates a previously much-used hollow-way.   Continue along this rising gravel track with coppice and bracken all around and super views over to your left, past several odd old oaks scattered to left and right.

A further 1/4 mile of slightly rising ridge walking with hazels, beeches, oaks and pines on both sides brings you to a more level section.   Then, the track bears left at a very boggy area.   Don't follow it around the corner but keep straight on, past a 'Bridlepath' notice to a half-gate and a stile in the fence which borders the woods.   Through the gate or over the stile, turn left to follow the left edge of the field until you see a large barn to your right.   Now, aim slightly to the right of its roof.   As you cross the field, you will see a gate in the far left corner with a mobile phone aerial over the fence on the left.

Go through the gate with a farm track enclosed between wire fences on your right into a wide concrete yard.   Bear right onto the high, wide and stony track between the LH fence and the RH ditch.

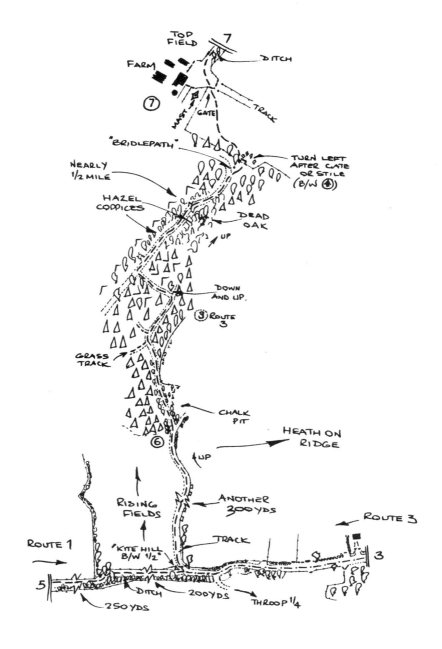

STAGE 7

PIDDLE WOOD TO SHITTERTON

ROUTES 1 AND 3: As you continue, long-distance views of Poole and the Bournemouth Overcliff flats come into view ahead, slightly left. Follow the 200 yards of wide track, with the ditch widening on your right, to a complicated junction of gates, fields and tracks. Standing in the middle of the junction, you can see Bere Regis down to your left. A track turns down to your right whilst there is one up to your left and another running into a field on your half-right. You don't want any of these. Instead, head straight on to the enclosed, wide and grass-verged track which is guarded by a barrier and a section of wooden fence. It has Jubilee Trail arrow. As you walk along the level, grassy track, you can see the cutting of the A35 Bere Regis by-pass as it skirts to the North of the town.

Suddenly, at a gate and a squeeze for pedestrians across your path, the fields end and the Great Heath begins again. The sudden change illustrates just how much difference was made by the hard work of claiming heathland for agriculture.

Go through the gate and begin another stroll across the gorse and heather-clad heath. In about 250 yards, you will see Turners Puddle Church and Toners Puddle farm down to your right. After just about another 100 yards, the track divides into two (with the right one returning in a loop to Turners Puddle). Take the left fork - for just 12 yards only - and then, at a 'Permissive Path' arrow-post, turn sharp left onto a heathy path which descends steeply through the bracken.

ROUTE 2: Having followed the Stage 2 map to here, you will soon see another gravel track coming in from your left at a Y-junction. A few paces *before* this fork junction, turn sharp right onto a 'Permissive Path' and follow the steeply-descending heathy path through the bracken.

ALL ROUTES: Follow the bending peaty path around the edge of a small Culpepper's Dish with a treacherous bog in the bottom. Over earth banks with a Permissive Path and a J/Tr arrow post and through a few silver birches, pass a smaller dish and go through another. Entering a mixed wood and coppice, the path meets another path from your right. Follow the LH fence to a half-gate with a J/Tr arrow on it. There is a 'Permissive Path' arrow on its other side. Also, a notice on the other side shows that these woods and some of the heath are part of a conservation grazing programme in conjunction with Turners Puddle Farm. Go through the gate and follow the descending track into a wide, banked hollow-way with holly and oaks in its banks.

Becoming steeper on a sharper fall, the trees close overhead into a shady tunnel with ferny banks and, after 1/4 mile of this descent, a hazel hedge leads you down past openings into fields on both sides to a T-junction of banked and unsigned Bridleways. Turn left and follow the hedged track down and round a right bend with a Footpath-arrow post on the left corner and with fields beyond the high banks on both sides.

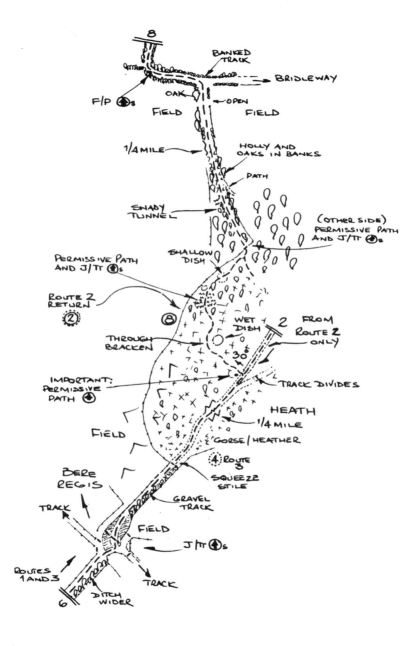

8

BANKED TRACK

BRIDLEWAY

F/P ④s

OAK

←OPEN

FIELD   FIELD

1/4 MILE

HOLLY AND OAKS IN BANKS

PATH

SHADY TUNNEL

(OTHER SIDE) PERMISSIVE PATH AND J/π ④s

SHALLOW DISH

PERMISSIVE PATH AND J/π ④s

ROUTE 2 RETURN ②

WET DISH

2 FROM ROUTE 2 ONLY

THROUGH BRACKEN

30

IMPORTANT: PERMISSIVE PATH ④

TRACK DIVIDES

HEATH 1/4 MILE

FIELD

GORSE/HEATHER

BERE REGIS

④ ROUTE 3

SQUEEZ STILE

TRACK

GRAVEL TRACK

FIELD

J/π ④s

ROUTES 1 AND 3

TRACK

6

DITCH WIDER

STAGE 8

SHITTERTON TO BERE REGIS

Keep following the track, past two more openings and past a right track opposite a left private gate.   Past two cottage gardens, you arrive in the road through the village of Shitterton.   A Footpath arrow post now confirms your arrival direction. Turn right and walk down the street of white painted and thatched cottages.

For your return into Bere Regis, there are THREE alternatives.

1. When you reach the LH bend at the white cottage facing you, a Footpath arrow next to the postbox shows the first possibility so I'll take you up there first although it isn't the best.   Walk up between the cottages and you'll emerge onto a wide, grassy area with an open field facing you.   Turn left and follow the path between the wire fence and the orchard on your left.   In a while, the Bere Stream joins you on your left and brings you to a footbridge bringing the 3rd alternative walkers from your left.   Keep straight on along the path.   Go to **1 and 3** below.

THE OTHERS: Go round the corner and follow the road between more cottages on your left and a tile-capped cob wall on the RH verge.   After Sitterton House and another thatched cottage on the right, go over the brick-parapetted bridge which spans the Bere Stream.

2. Walk up the road for the direct route into West Street, Bere Regis and ignore everything that follows.

3. I'm going this way.   After the bridge, turn right onto the gravel path over the open green between the far left new houses and the hedged Bere Stream on your right.   This level stroll brings you to a duck-board above the boggy ground and a footbridge over the stream.   Cross the bridge and the duck-board on the far side and turn left to join the others from the first alternative on a path between the field and the stream.   Go to **1 and 3** below.

1 AND 3. In a few more yards, the path turns down to a stile with a Footpath arrow (on the other side).   Go over the stile into a very long meadow with a banked hedge on your right and the Bere Stream running towards the watercress beds on your left.   This is a fine stroll through the water meadow with good views of the Church of St John the Baptist ahead of you.   Turn to Stage 1 map to finish.

*CHURCH OF ST JOHN THE BAPTIST: There has been a church on this site since Saxon times but the present building **only** dates back to 1050AD.   It was widened in the mid-12thC and lengthened in the 13thC.   Again, the South side was widened in the 14thC and the North side in the 15thC to its present size. That is when the magnificent, painted and gilded oak nave roof was built.   The church leaflet will expand further on the details of the twelve full sized carved apostles but they seem to be in alphabetical order, starting in the North West corner.   There are some fine brasses inside.   The large chained hooks in the porch were once fitted to the ends of very long poles.   They were used for pulling down thatched roofs in the face of advancing fires.   That is the source of the expression still used in modern demolition when a building is said to be 'pulled down' even though it is demolished with a huge iron ball or sledgehammers.*

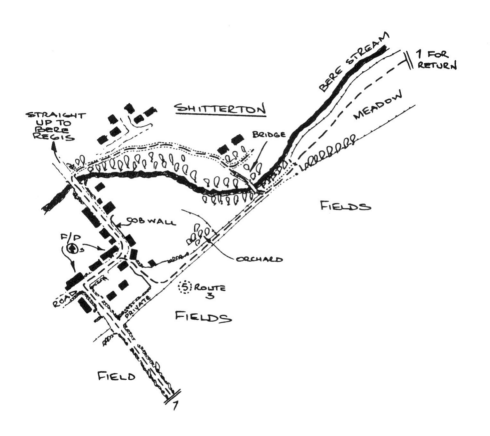

PART NINE - SUTTON POYNTZ

INTRODUCTION

Holidaymakers to the coastal resort of Weymouth (made famous through the patronage of King George III after his first visit in 1789) and to the Caravan parks of Preston have enjoyed the backdrop of Chalbury Hill Fort and White Horse Hill for many years. However, few have ventured onto the ridge for an airy ramble or to view Weymouth Bay and the Isle of Portland from its barrow studded heights or explored the lovely village of Osmington

Sutton Poyntz lies North of the A353 Weymouth to Osmington road and both walks begin at the junction of the minor roads to 'Bincombe' and 'Sutton Poyntz'. The road is wider and the parking easier in Plaisters Lane, just after the signpost to 'Bincombe' and the telephone box at Ref SY706837 on O S Map No. 194. Alternatively, you can park by the pond in the village near where the 'A' bus turns round in Silver Street for its return to Weymouth - at Ref SY707839 and walk down to the start. Excepting Sundays and Bank Holidays, there are plenty of buses to and from Sutton Poyntz and it's only a 13 minute ride so you can leave the car in Weymouth if you wish.

In the Domesday Book simply as *Sutone*, the land was owned by King William I. Hundreds of Dorset mills listed in the Domesday Book have disappeared since 1086. Conversely, a water mill was built in Sutton Poyntz about 1820 but none was recorded in 1086. Sutton simply means 'South Town'. 'Poyntz' recalls the Poyntz family who were ancient landowners and lords of the vills of Sutton and nearby Preston. In the time of Edward II, Sir Nicholas Poyntz gave Preston to Sir John de Newburgh from nearby Winfrith Newburgh on his daughter's marriage.

THE ALTERNATIVES

There is just one walk here, chosen from many and I'm sure there will be some more in a later book. The walk climbs up to Chalbury hill fort before enjoying a superb 2 mile ridge walk along part of the Inland Coast Path with wonderful views over Weymouth Bay and the Isle of Portland. From a spot above the famous White Horse, a descending farm track leads to Church Lane, Osmington for a visit to the lovely St Osmund's church. Then a pleasant stroll through sheep meadows, parallel to the slopes of White Horse Hill, leads back to Sutton Poyntz.

ROUTE: Total distance 4.3/4 miles.

	STAGE	MILES	TOTAL MILES
1	Sutton Poyntz to Chalbury Hill Fort	1	1
2	Chalbury Hill Fort to Four Parishes	1	2
3	Four Parishes to Osmington	1	3
4	Osmington to Sutton Poyntz	1.75	**4.75**

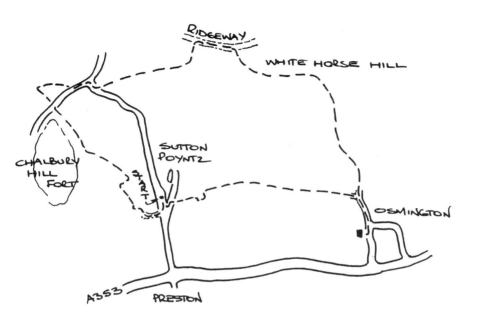

Chalbury Hill Fort from top field - Page 132

STAGE 1

SUTTON POYNTZ TO CHALBURY HILL FORT

From the wider part of Plaisters Lane, almost opposite Old Bincombe Lane, walk down towards the Y-junction and keep going, past the telephone box on the opposite corner with Brook Mead.   Or, if you are coming down from the duck-pond, join Plaisters Lane at the Y-junction.

After the telephone box, turn right into Puddledock Lane.   Follow the lane, with a stream in the trees on your left at first and with houses on your right.   Very soon, the lane turns sharp right at the Old Dairy House with 'The Puddledocks' converted dairy buildings on your left.   Now the lane turns sharp left again.   In a few yards, turn right at a 'Public Footpath' sign and join a chalk track with grass up the middle and with hedges, trees and ditches on either side.   In about 100 yards, you will reach a gate with three Footpath arrows on a post.   Follow the clear track straight on across an open field, rising only slightly towards the opposite hedge.   Through the opening in the hedge and into the next field, follow the RH hedge as the track rises more steeply with Chalbury ahead of you.   The path then turns sharp right to follow the hedge along the slopes of the hill.

There is no public access onto Chalbury hill fort from this side.   However, as this is quite a short walk, you may wish to visit the fort on your way and I will tell you how to get there when you are closer to the access point.   Chalbury stands on the North end of Rimbury ridge which splits a valley running North from Weymouth Bay.   It was excavated in 1939 by a Miss Whitley and was found to date back to the Iron Age although it was later occupied as a Romano-British settlement.

Now, keep following the RH hedge with a steep bank down into a ditch, and go through an opening in the next facing hedge which comes steeply down from the trees on the East slope of the hill.   At the end of this undulating field, turn left and keep following the field edge, now increasingly steep, to the top corner.   On the way up this field, you may permitted a few stops to have your first sight of the sea over on the left.   The Footpath-arrowed stile in the top corner has a remnant of a stone wall on its left.   Over the stile, don't follow the LH fence but bear slightly right and cross the rising ground for about 500 yards, aiming for a distant stile at first.   As you progress, you will see that the stile is in a distant field but the stile you really want will have come into view, just to the right of the single stone barn and to the left of the hill scarp on your right.   Over the crest of the hill, walk up to the far right corner, close by the scarp on the right.

The low banks which run across the hill as you progress are remnants of medieval strip lynchets and are not connected with occupation of the fort.

Here, you will find a Footpath-arrowed stile out onto the verge alongside the top road.   You now have several choices: If you would like to have a tramp over Chalbury before continuing on the circular walk, the access stile is 1/2 mile down the road to your left.   If you would like to continue the walk immediately, you can either walk along the verge for 250 yards or avoid the road by crossing over and slogging up the steep hill opposite before returning to the road 250 yards away. Assuming you will want to keep off the road, cross over and go over two stiles which lead you onto the steep slope alongside a wire fence.

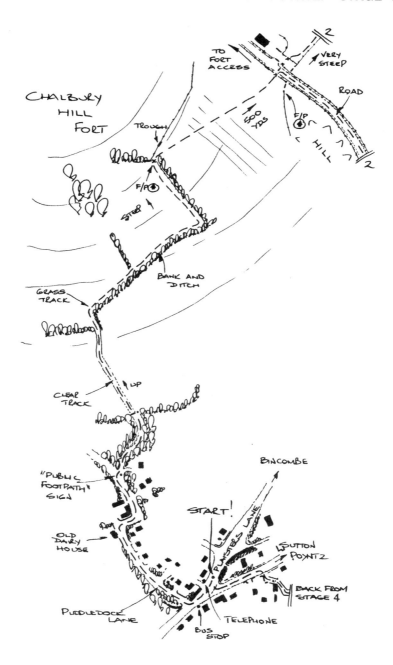

CHALBURY
HILL
FORT

TO
FORT
ACCESS

VERY
STEEP

ROAD

TROUGH

600
YDS

F/P

HILL

2

F/P⊙

STEP

BANK AND
DITCH

GRASS
TRACK

CLEAR
TRACK

UP

BINCOMBE

"PUBLIC
FOOTPATH"
SIGN

START!

SUTTON
POYNTZ

OLD
DAIRY
HOUSE

BACK FROM
STAGE 4

PUDDLEDOCK
LANE

TELEPHONE

BUS
STOP

STAGE 2

CHALBURY HILL FORT TO FOUR PARISHES

Go straight up the hill, stopping only to fight for breath and to admire the views behind you. At the top, go over the stile. Keep to the edge of this elongated field, crossing an extinct track which came through the stone gate posts on your left. At the top of this field, there are Bridleway and Footpath arrows on the other side of the gate but you don't need to know this because you shouldn't be going through it. Instead, stop and admire the views over Weymouth Bay to Portland before following the descending grass track for 400 yards to a gate with signs for 'Bridleway Inland Route Bincombe 3/4' and 'Inland Route Footpath Osmington 2.3/4'. Go back out onto the road you recently crossed 250 yards away.

Turn left and walk past the stone buildings on your right. The verge disappears for a few yards before you find a grassy refuge at a junction with two Footpath arrows and the Sutton Poyntz road on your right. The signpost finial declares that you are at 'Coombe Valley 697844'. Turn right and walk up the banked road to the brow of the hill.

Go through the gate on your left with the sign 'Inland Coast Path Osmington 2.3/4'. Join a chalk and grass track for the start of a super ridge walk with lovely views over Preston and Weymouth Bay. After the first 500 yards of slightly rising path, and passing a round barrow on your left, you reach a gate with a Bridleway arrow. There is a boundary stone against the stone wall on the left. *This tells you that you are crossing into the Borough of Weymouth and Melcombe Regis. You have only been in the Parish of Bincombe since the strip lynchets' field and the boundaries get more complicated later.*

Through the gate, the little path on your right runs straight back down to Sutton Poyntz but it's too early to leave the ridge. From here, there are good views of the coast ridge that runs parallel with Chesil Beach towards West Bay and, if you are lucky, there may be a few dozen goldfinches flitting about. Keep strolling along the ridge, with more barrows on your left and ahead. Soon, you arrive at a gorse-clad valley on the right with another path which goes to Sutton Poyntz. *This valley is the source of the River Jordan. No, not that one. This one runs out into the sea at Bowleaze Cove.* Past the head of the valley, go through a gate with an 'Inland Coast Path' pointer. There is a group of three round barrows in this next field. When the stone wall and fence turn left, follow them, passing a ruined stone barn on your way to a gate.

Through the gateway, you are on the White Horse Hill Ridgeway. Another fingerpost sends you right along the 'Inland Coast Path'. As you walk along the wide, chalk and grass track, the villages down on your front left (at 46º NE) are Broadmayne and West Knighton. When the track bears left to 'Broadmayne 1.1/4' at another fingerpost, turn right onto the rising grassy track, signed for 'Osmington 1.1/2'. *Here you are at the junction of four parishes - Bincombe, Broadmayne, Poxwell and Weymouth. The erratic boulder on your left is probably an old marker placed here for the purpose.*

134

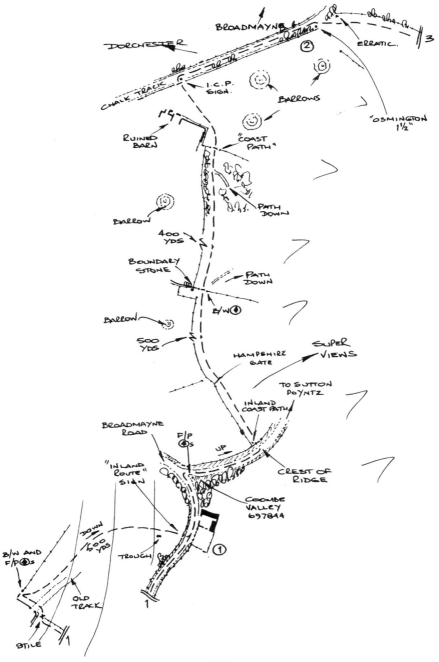

BROADMAYNE

DORCHESTER

②

ERRATIC.

CHALK TRACK

I.C.P. SIGN.

BARROWS

"OSMINGTON 1½"

RUINED BARN

"COAST PATH"

BARROW

PATH DOWN

400 YDS

BOUNDARY STONE

PATH DOWN

E/W ④

BARROW

500 YDS

HAMPSHIRE GATE

SUPER VIEWS

TO SUTTON POYNTZ

INLAND COAST PATH

BROADMAYNE ROAD

F/P ④s

UP

CREST OF RIDGE

"INLAND ROUTE" SIGN

COOMBE VALLEY 697844

DOWN 600 YDS

B/W AND F/P ④s

TROUGH

①

OLD TRACK

STILE

1

1

135

STAGE 3

FOUR PARISHES TO OSMINGTON

Still enjoying the high level walking, there are two more barrows on your right and the town down on your reverse left (330º NNW) is Dorchester.   After the barrows, the O.S. trig point plinth stands at 158m (519ft) on East Hill.   Keep straight on to the next gate.   You are now passing into the parish of Osmington.   The path to your right, signed 'To the White Horse' takes you down to Sutton Poyntz by a very steep, chalky ascent through gorse bushes, alongside the Horse's tail and through hawthorns lower down.

Keep straight on again, signed for 'Poxwell'.   The track now slopes slightly downhill and affords views over Thomas Hardy's 'Great Heath' on your left and to Osmington ahead on your right.   At the next gate, take the sunken chalk track which descends at an angle on your right.   It is signed for 'Osmington 1' and 'West Lulworth 8'.   This is a long descent, sometimes between high banks and sometimes with gorse and hawthorns on the sides but with great views over the lovely patchwork of fields.   At the bottom, the route runs past a thicket on your right before becoming a wide, descending, hedge-bordered track.   At its end, there is a gate and a stile with a Bridleway arrow.

At the next left bend, there is a good view over the gate on the corner back to the White Horse and beyond to Chalbury hill fort.   *The figure is George II but this was added to the ancient White Horse which is of a similar date to the Westbury and Uffington white horses.*   Now, keep going along the track.

St Osmund's Parish Church, Osmington - Page 138

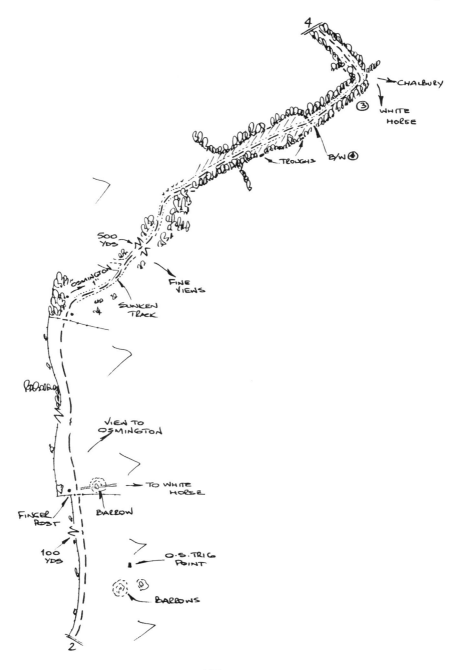

4

CHALBURY

③ WHITE HORSE

B/W ④

TROUGHS

500 YDS

FINE VIEWS

OSMINGTON

SUNKEN TRACK

VIEW TO OSMINGTON

TO WHITE HORSE

BARROW

FINGER POST

100 YDS

O.S. TRIG POINT

BARROWS

2

STAGE 4

OSMINGTON TO SUTTON POYNTZ

The last stretch of the enclosed track is quite level before rising and passing a gate on the right with a Bridleway arrow and an 'Inland Route' sign. When you reach a well and pump on the right corner, the lane becomes tarmac and ascends past Charity Farm on your left. *Originally, the house was a 16thC long-house with the dwelling and cattle byre under one roof. It was purchased in 1665 (the year of the Black Death) by the Corporation of Melcombe Regis with a bequest from Sir Samuel Mico. The rent from the farm was used to pay for the relief of the poor. Since then, the house has been much altered and partly rebuilt.*

Take note of the well because you will be turning off here after your visit to St Osmund's. When you reach the stone- mullion windowed cottage on the corner of 'Church Lane' with 'Village Street' on your left, keep straight up the hill. Just beyond the row of mixed thatch and slate cottages, go through the lych gate onto the pathway up to the church. *The stone and slate Parish Church of St Osmund stands on a very ancient site. A chancel arch within the present chancel dates back to about 1200. The tower is 15thC but most of the church was rebuilt in 1846. The stone wall on the right of the churchyard is the remaining part of the 17thC Osmington Manor House. Very little remains to be seen but the South wall which faces the churchyard has the original mullioned windows (one sealed) and a sunken door which leads into the ruin and the garden which it occupies.*

After your visit, return to the well which you saw earlier. Go up the hedge-lined track which runs to your left (coming down the hill), signed 'Sutton Poyntz 1.1/2'. The track bends somewhat before arriving at a gateway with no arrows ahead of you. Go through the gate and follow the RH hedge until it turns away to the right. Then, cross the field, turning slightly downwards towards the far corner (278º W).

After 500 yards, the gate in the hedge opens onto a wide track which you cross over to another gate in the wire fence. Both gates have Footpath arrows. Through the second gate, aim for Chalbury hill fort. You are surrounded by hills and ridges but there is a lovely airy feel about this wide valley route. This field is about 600 yards long and, as you progress, veer a little towards your right to find a Footpath-arrowed stile in the far RH corner hedges. The remains of the stone walls and the vertical stone slab are more boundary markers as you return from Osmington parish into the old Weymouth and Melcombe Regis Parish.

Now, keep to the high hedge and trees which follow a stream on your right for about 400 yards. Go through an opening in the hedge into the next field and, after another 400 yards, you arrive at a track. Zig-zag left/right into a small field. At a Footpath arrow on the corner of a small fenced enclosure on your right, turn down to cross the stream and go through the Footpath arrowed wicket gate to the left of another farm gate. Follow the clear path to a stile which takes you into an enclosed path through gardens.

When you emerge onto the road at a confirmation 'Public Footpath' sign, the duck-pond is up the road, past the mill on your right and the telephone box at the start of the walk in Plaisters Lane is down on your left. So, off you go, back to your car or your bus or to partake of a little refreshment at the Springhead Inn.

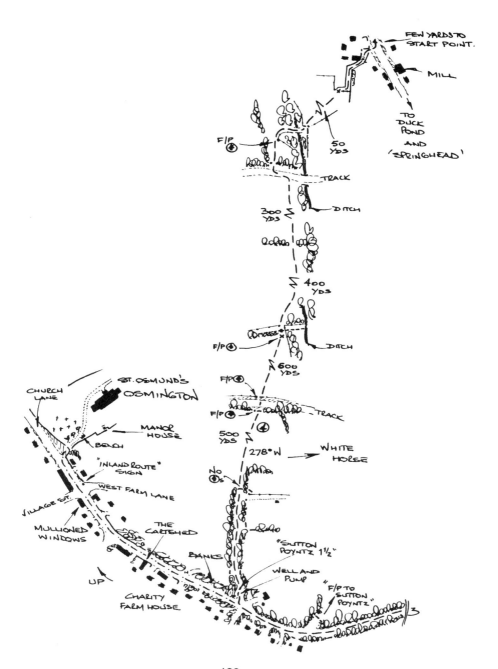

IN CONCLUSION

This book was researched throughout an entire year and, whilst some of the walks were enjoyed during the sunniest days imaginable, others were researched during the shorter, colder days of winter. I must say that, apart from the long-distance views being less spectacular during damp, overcast days, the feelings of solitude are considerably heightened. Some of the finest days were the crisp, frosty ones of January and, if you wrap up warm and take plenty of hot drinks, you can enjoy the bracing air of the Dorset downs whatever the weather. Another bonus is the low angle of the Winter sun. Although it may cause you to shade your eyes at times, these are circular walks so you are only walking towards the sun for a short part of each excursion. But, if you are interested in discovering Dorset's past, there's nothing like a low sun to show you the ancient ridges and furrows of our ancestors' fields or the bumps and hollows that show where a village once stood, maybe in the first centuries of the first millennium as on the Piddletrenthide walk. Then again, a sunny stroll in shorts and big boots takes a lot of beating, especially if you have a favourite watering hole waiting for your return.

Whilst working on these walks, I enjoyed the Purbeck coast again and found the inland route around Harman's Cross quite enchanting with its farms, its lovely views and its old houses. The area around Sturminster Newton called me back again. I loved visiting some favourite villages and enjoyed a new stroll through Piddles Wood. Sturminster Marshall was somewhere I hadn't visited before and the riverside stroll and the visit to Spetisbury Rings hill fort was a revelation - so much so that I included another walk that calls at Spetisbury Rings as well. A circular walk based on Throop Mill had suggested itself many times in the past but this is the first time I have found the space to include it. I'm sure you'll enjoy the tranquillity so close to Bournemouth's sprawl. Wimborne Minster and Bere Regis both provided two of the longer walks (and short ones as well) and, for those who have never visited Hardy's Heath, the Puddles and Culpepper's Dish will demand your return. Last, but definitely not least, the White Horse Hill above Sutton Poyntz offers tremendous views, not only over Weymouth Bay to Portland but over the North side to the high downs beyond Dorchester and into the Blackmore Vale. What an absolute treat.

As I said in an earlier book, this guide will lead you to some sublime countryside which will provide you with memories that you will cherish for many years to come.

ACKNOWLEDGEMENTS

As always, thanks to my wife Janet for joining me in checking some of the new walks We were rewarded by sightings of deer, buzzards, a young cormorant, snowdrops and primroses on the Bere Regis walk in February. Jan's lunches have given many surprises and they have been enjoyed beneath the blazing sun and whilst sheltering from downpours in the most beautiful churchyards.

My visits to Bournemouth and Dorchester Reference Libraries have become less frequent as my birthday, Christmas and anytime presents have become mostly standardised into RCHM volumes or anything old about Dorset. Nevertheless, I would like to thank everyone who has helped me out at those establishments and in the Rights of Way Sections of the various Council's Offices.

BIBLIOGRAPHY

History and Antiquities of the County of Dorset: Rev John Hutchins 1861 - 64
Inventory of Historical Monuments in the County of Dorset: H.M.S.O. 1970
Highways and Byways of Dorset: Sir Frederick Treves 1914
Dorset Churches: Sir Owen Morshead: Dorset Historic Churches Trust 1976
The Place Names of Dorset - Parts 2 and 3: A D Mills of the English Place Names
Society - Edited by K Cameron.
Portrait of Dorset: Ralph Wightman: Robert Hale
Inside Dorset: Monica Hutchings 1964
Geology Explained in Dorset: John W Perkins: David and Charles
Purbeck Shop: Eric Benfield: Ensign Publications
Cranborne Chase: Desmond Hawkins: Victor Gollancz 1980
The Domesday Book: Edited by Thomas Hinde: Guild Publishing

INDEX

PERSONAL LOG

PERSONAL LOG